GET OVER YOURSELF

THANKS !

James

GET OVER YOURSELF

Dr. James R. Love Sr.

CREATION HOUSE
H O U S E
A STRANG COMPANY

GET OVER YOURSELF by Dr. James R. Love Sr.
Published by Creation House
A Strang Company
600 Rinehart Road
Lake Mary, Florida 32746
www.creationhouse.com

Unless otherwise noted, all Scripture quotations are from the New King James Version of the Bible. Copyright © 1979, 1980, 1982 by Thomas Nelson, Inc., publishers. Used by permission.

Scripture quotations marked AMP are from the Amplified Bible. Old Testament copyright © 1965, 1987 by the Zondervan Corporation. The Amplified New Testament copyright © 1954, 1958, 1987 by the Lockman Foundation. Used by permission.

Scripture quotations marked KJV are from the King James Version of the Bible.

Scripture quotations marked NAS are from the New American Standard Bible, Copyright © 1960, 1962, 1963, 1968, 1971, 1972, 1973, 1975, 1977, 1995 by the Lockman Foundation. Used by permission. (www.Lockman.org)

Scripture quotations marked NEB are from the New English Bible. Copyright © 1961, 1970 by the Delegates of the Oxford University Press and the Syndics of the Cambridge University Press. Used by permission.

Cover design by Terry Clifton

Library of Congress Control Number: 2006921024
International Standard Book Number: 1-59979-007-6

First Edition

06 07 08 09 10 — 987654321
Printed in the United States of America

The apostle Paul said in Romans 12:3, "For I say, through the grace given to me, to everyone who is among you, not to think of himself more highly than he ought to think, but to think soberly, as God has dealt to each one a measure of faith" (NKJV). This is the ultimate purpose of this book—to apply this to your life.

ACKNOWLEDGMENTS

I PROBABLY WOULDN'T HAVE taken the time to write this book if it hadn't been for my wife who encouraged me to do so. She is my biggest fan and sharpest critic! I also want to thank the wonderful people who God has allowed me to pastor, Faith Tabernacle United Holy Church of America in Washington, DC. I specifically want to give my profoundest appreciation to Minister LaDorothy Pittman for assisting me in editing and typing the early manuscripts. LaDorothy, thank you just doesn't seem enough to convey my deepest appreciation for your titanic efforts in this project. May God richly bless you!

CONTENTS

INTRODUCTION

EVEN THE CASUAL reader of the Gospels must observe that the central theme in Jesus' preaching was the kingdom of God. Matthew 4:17 states, "From that time Jesus began to preach, and to say, Repent: for the kingdom of heaven is at hand" (KJV). Yet, our understanding of this phrase has often been very different from what Jesus intended. We are confused about such issues as whether the kingdom is a present reality or a future hope. Is the kingdom the same as the church? Is the kingdom of heaven synonymous with the kingdom of God, or are they different?

Still, humankind has identified human hopes for a heavenly bliss on earth with the kingdom of God. These hopes have been at odds with the doctrine Jesus espoused. Often they are inconsistent with each other; yet, far too frequently, what is enunciated as God's kingdom is nothing more than the offspring of contemporary social or political thought. Others have relegated the kingdom of God to the future, thus removing it from any present relevance.

I've titled this book: *Get Over Yourself: Purposeful Kingdom Living in a Me-Centered World.* The gist of this idea revolves around the central message of Jesus, which is the kingdom of God and its practical demands upon every aspect of a Christian's lifestyle. Much of what I say will address the need for selflessness in contrast to a Christian culture that has become peculiarly me-centered. I provide a genteel corrective to the pervasive view that Christianity is about God meeting my needs, my wants, and my concerns. I hasten to add that all these have their place with balance. Too much of our culture focuses upon the individual: "It's all about me; I am the captain of my ship, the master of my fate," so they say. I contend that the problem with humankind is that living outside the kingdom we've become naturally selfish, self-sufficient, and self-centered.

Moreover, in this book I will specifically show the reader through relevant stories and poignant illustrations how to "get over yourself," and how to fully experience the blessings of God in his or her life.

I believe that this book idea would be particularly appealing to a young Christian who really desires to mature in his or her walk with Jesus Christ. However, I believe this book will also appeal to any Christian in a general sort of way because I will address those hindrances that impair intimacy with Jesus.

How is this book different from what is already in bookstores? In my survey of the Christian landscape, I have concluded that too much of what now passes for Christianity is me-centered, consumeristic, and personality fixated. Therefore, I am very concerned that we have settled for a cheap version of Christianity that placates "me." We have lost focus of the eternal; our eyes are gazed upon our needs being satisfied right now!

The word *kingdom* occurs approximately one hundred sixty times in the New Testament. The word *king* means "a sovereign who rules" and the suffix *-dom* is an abbreviation of the word "domain" or "territory." Thus, in the simplest form, the word *kingdom* means "rule of God." The kingdom of God, then, is the realm over which God reigns. It should be noted that the realm referred to is God's rule in both heaven and earth.

Is the kingdom of God a present reality or a future hope? In responding to this question, it is important to understand that the kingdom of God is essentially the rule of God; His reign and divine sovereignty in action. His reign, however, is manifested in several realms, and the Gospels do speak of entering into the kingdom both today and tomorrow. Therefore, God's reign manifests itself both in the present and in the future. Luke 17:20–21 states, "Now having been questioned by the Pharisees as to when the kingdom of God was coming, He answered them and said, 'The kingdom of God is not coming with signs to be observed; nor will they say, 'Look, here it is!' or, 'There it is!' For behold, the kingdom of God is in your midst" (NAS). In effect, Jesus was stating that the kingdom of God is not coming with any fanfare, but is already a present reality.

It may be compared to a mustard seed (Matthew 13:31–32); insignificant in appearance, yet, its power and influence are destined to dominate the whole world. Isaiah 2:2 states, "Now it shall come to pass in the latter days That the mountain of the LORD's house Shall be established on the top of the mountains, And shall be exalted above the hills; And all nations shall flow to it."

Yet, at the same time, the kingdom is an inheritance that God will bestow upon His people when Christ comes in glory. Note what Matthew 25:34 says, "Then the King will say to those on His right, 'Come, you who are blessed of My Father, inherit the kingdom prepared for you from the foundation of the world" (NAS). Also, the parable of the tares explained by Jesus in Matthew 13:32–43 makes it clear that the kingdom has a future consummation.

In our attempt to introduce the kingdom of God, there remains one question that we must give attention to—is the kingdom of God synonymous with the church? Some Bible teachers have so identified the church with the kingdom that there is really no distinction between the two. They espouse the notion that as the church grows and expands throughout the earth, in effect, the kingdom of God is doing likewise. However, is the kingdom of God nothing more than a clone of the church? It is my observation that although there is a relationship between the two, the kingdom is neither the church nor a clone of the church. Along this line, my thinking has been influenced by the late theologian, George E. Ladd.

He makes the following distinction between the church and the kingdom:

1. The church is not the kingdom. The church is the people of the kingdom, never the kingdom itself. The kingdom is the rule of God; the church is a society of men.

2. The kingdom created the church.

3. The church witnesses to the kingdom.

4. The church is the instrument of the kingdom.

5. The church is the custodian of the kingdom.

While there is an inseparable relationship between the kingdom and the church, they are not to be identified. The kingdom takes its point of departure from God; the church from men. The kingdom is God's reign and the realm in which the blessings of His reign are experienced; the church is the fellowship of those who have experienced God's reign and enter into the enjoyment of its blessings. The kingdom creates the church, works through the church, and is proclaimed in the world by the church. There can be no kingdom without a church—those who have acknowledged God's rule—and there can be no church without God's kingdom; but they remain two distinguishable concepts: the rule of God and the fellowship of men.[1]

I will have much more to say about this later in chapter one.

Resident Aliens and Pilgrims

I have come to believe that one of the great dangers to the modern Christian, especially in these post-modern times, is the loss of an eternal perspective. I have, and I am sure you have too, heard believers say, "So and so is too heavenly-minded to be any earthly good." Well, it is this kind of thinking that has slowly crept into the church and is the reason why too many believers have been secularized. The apostle Paul, in Colossians 3:1–4, essentially says we need to have our focus more on eternal things than upon things on this earth.

It is my contention that the general culture has so influenced and thus secularized Christians that we have settled for the temporal instead of the eternal. I ask you: When was the last time you heard a sermon on heaven? Or sang a hymn or praise chorus that spoke of the transcended attributes of God? It is this lack of an eternal perspective that has hindered our comprehension of the kingdom. Why? Because the kingdom requires that I get over myself and thus focus upon the transcended King of kings, Jesus Christ!

Now, I am not suggesting that Christians withdraw from engaging the general culture. On the contrary! I believe they must engage this culture with the truth of the gospel, apologetically, coherently, and compassionately. But we, similarly, must recognize that this culture has a reality; a worldview; that is fundamentally antithetical to the gospel. Therefore, I must realize that this world is not my home. The apostle Paul says in Philippians 3:20, "For our citizenship is in heaven, from which also we eagerly wait for a Savior, the Lord Jesus Christ" (NAS). As a citizen of the kingdom of Jesus Christ I must live as though I am a resident alien within the context of this culture.

In conclusion, I believe the kingdom is present today, yet it has a future culmination. I think the phrase coined by one biblical scholar, "The kingdom now, but not yet," accurately captures this proposition. I must hasten to add that some Bible teachers see the kingdom as entirely future, e.g. those who hold a dispensational view of eschatology, or others who hold the view that the kingdom is present in various human social agendas, e.g. those who hold a more liberal Protestant view. I categorically reject both of the aforementioned views.

Fundamentally, I believe the kingdom ought to affect our

relationships within and without the church. I will, on this point, discuss Jesus' admonition to "love one another" and His scathing rebuke of those who are judgmental. Further, I will discuss what it means to be "born again" into the kingdom and how trouble and tribulation are actually doorways into the kingdom rule of God in an individual's life. Fundamentally, the clarion call of the kingdom is that we learn what it means to get over ourselves!

In addition, I will discuss practical principles for daily kingdom living. It is important for you to know that there are laws of the kingdom just as there are laws in the physical world. The law of gravity is an obvious example of a physical law. Similarly, kingdom laws are spiritual principles that are just as real as the physical laws. In this section, I'll present short vignettes of various principles of the kingdom and their practical application. We will review such principles as envy, jealousy anger, and forgiveness, just to name a few.

I believe you will find this book both devotionally encouraging as well as exegetically sound.

Chapter 1

GOD HAS A KINGDOM

Christianity did not come in order to develop the heroic virtues in the individual, but rather to remove self centeredness and establish love.[1]

—SOREN KIERKGAARD

And I will give you the keys of the kingdom of heaven, and whatever you bind on earth will be bound in heaven, and whatever you loose on earth will be loosed in heaven.

—MATTHEW 16:19

Do not fear, little flock, for it is your Father's good pleasure to give you the kingdom.

—LUKE 12:32

And He said to them, "To you it has been given to know the mystery of the kingdom of God; but to those who are outside, all things come in parables."

—MARK 4:11

Did You Know That Our God Has a Kingdom?

I find that there are too many Christians who either don't know this, so their lives aren't governed by the authority of the King; or they know of the kingdom, yet they choose to govern their own lives as if it doesn't matter. But God does have a kingdom and He expects those who know Him to govern their lives by His kingdom principles. I believe that in order to understand what the kingdom is all about one must first start with the very

1

first verse of the very first book of the Bible—Genesis. It is here we meet the Sovereign of the universe whose realm, rule, and regency is described. By realm, I mean the expanse or scope of His rule. God's rule is transcendent; His rule is not only over the physical world but also over the unseen spiritual world. God existed before all creation, He expands beyond it, and by virtue of having created it He encompasses all of it. By rule, I mean His power or reign in which He does exercise the divine prerogatives as sovereign ruler. This power to rule is seen in the exercise of His will, His Word, and His work.

- His will comes to pass.
- His words are spoken with authority.
- His works manifest His awesome power.

By *regency*, I mean His authority to rule by reason of His preexistence and awesome holiness; He is the uncreated one, the un-beginning one who was before there is and is before there was. God's intent in creation was to express His love to humankind so that humankind would enjoy fellowship with Him.

Adam, by an act of his free will, chose to disobey and, through his act, the entire world was plunged into disorder and chaos. Jesus came to announce that God's kingdom has now invalidated this present order, and He is inaugurating a new order!

Psalm 145:11–13 says, "They shall speak of the glory of Your kingdom, And talk of Your power, To make known to the sons of men His mighty acts, And the glorious majesty of His kingdom. Your kingdom is an everlasting kingdom, And Your dominion endures throughout all generations."

What Is the Kingdom of God?

The modern understanding of "kingdom" as basically that of a territory or realm misses the Biblical idea completely. For example, we are all aware of the Arab nations or England, which have specific territories. And they have a monarch; a king or queen. *The American Heritage Dictionary* defines the word *kingdom* as, "The rank, quality, state, or attributes of a king; royal authority; rulership."[2] The primary meaning of the word *kingdom* in Greek (*basileia*) and Hebrew (*malkuth*) is rulership or government. Thus, the idea of the kingdom of God is the sovereign rule or government of God.

Allow me to illustrate using Luke 19:11–27. Historically, around 40 B.C., Herod the Great went to Rome to receive authorization to be king over Palestine. He was granted such authority.

The point is he had to obtain permission to be the king. His rulership was sanctioned by the ruling might of the Roman Empire.

Now, if you were asked what the central message of Jesus is, what would your response be: love, hell, salvation, God? Actually, Jesus spent more time teaching about the kingdom of God. Read Matthew 4:17, Mark 1:15, and Luke 4:43, 9:2. Also, the apostles in Acts 19:8 taught the kingdom of God.

Is This Kingdom a Future Reality or Is It a Present Reality?

Some Bible teachers say this kingdom is a future reality, and others say it's a present one. The Bible seems to teach that the kingdom is present right now in seed form, yet it also has a future reality of culmination.

A present reality

> Now when He was asked by the Pharisees when the kingdom of God would come, He answered them and said, 'The kingdom of God does not come with observation; nor will they say, "See here!" or "See there!" For indeed, the kingdom of God is within you.
>
> —LUKE 17:20–21

> But if I cast out demons by the Spirit of God, surely the kingdom of God has come upon you.
>
> —MATTHEW 12:28

A future reality

> Then the King will say to those on His right hand, "Come, you blessed of My Father, inherit the kingdom prepared for you from the foundation of the world."
>
> —MATTHEW 25:34

> For so an entrance will be supplied to you abundantly into the everlasting kingdom of our Lord and Savior Jesus Christ.
>
> —2 PETER 1:11

One writer said that the kingdom is "now but not yet." I agree with this statement.

Now How Does One Enter Into This Kingdom of God and What Are Its Demands?

1. You can't *see* the kingdom until you're born again (John 3:1–5).

2. You can't *receive* the kingdom until you become childlike (Matt. 18:1–4).

The kingdom of God will demand of you:

1. Complete surrender
2. Total submission
3. Unquestioned obedience
4. Radical abandonment

I believe that the kingdom of God is His breaking into our world with His glory and power. The kingdom brings comfort to those in distress and distress to those who are comfortable.

Is There a Difference Between the Kingdom of God and the Kingdom of Heaven?

Dr. C. L. Scofield taught that the kingdom of heaven is God's rule over the hearts of men on the earth, whereas, the kingdom of God is universal, incorporating man as well as the angelic hosts.[3] (See particularly the 1909 edition of the *Scofield Reference Bible*, page 972)

Read: Matthew 12:28; 19:23–24; 21:31, 43.

In a point of fact, there is no difference between "The kingdom of God" and "The kingdom of heaven." The above referenced scriptures confirm this assertion. Even *The New Scofield Reference and Bible* 1967 edition acknowledges this position, although it states on page 1002 that it "is to be distinguished from it in some instances."[4] In my opinion, this is still incorrect!

We Are Resident Aliens

There are natural laws that govern the visible physical world, such as:

- Law of gravity—things that go up must come down
- Law of aerodynamics—speed and lift allow planes to fly
- Law of thermodynamics—in physics, the relationship between heat and other forms of energy

There are also laws that govern the invisible spiritual world. To be a person who lives in the kingdom is to recognize the laws that govern the kingdom. Jesus said in Mark 4:11, "To you it has been given to know the mystery of the kingdom of God." So, because we are so preoccupied with ourselves we have neglected the practical reality of what it means to live under the rulership of God.

I believe we must begin to see ourselves as pilgrims who are just passing through this world to the real world of the kingdom. The older saints were correct when they would enunciate that "this world is not my home, so I won't hold on to anything down here too tightly." Thus, to live as a citizen of the kingdom of God is to actually live as a resident alien now. It is on this point that I want to hang my argument. You see, until you possess the kingdom of Jesus Christ operating within your life, you will never learn the secret to getting over yourself. It is axiomatic: only when you learn how to humbly submit to the kingdom rule of Jesus are you capable of getting over yourself.

Chapter 2

EMPLOYEE'S HANDBOOK OF THE KINGDOM

—————⟫◦⟪—————

Brooks become crooked from taking the path of least resistance. So do people.[1]

—HAROLD KOHN

And seeing the multitudes, He went up on a mountain, and when He was seated His disciples came to Him. Then He opened His mouth and taught them, saying: "Blessed are the poor in spirit, For theirs is the kingdom of heaven. Blessed are those who mourn, For they shall be comforted. Blessed are the meek, For they shall inherit the earth. Blessed are those who hunger and thirst for righteousness, For they shall be filled. Blessed are the merciful, For they shall obtain mercy. Blessed are the pure in heart, For they shall see God. Blessed are the peacemakers, For they shall be called sons of God. Blessed are those who are persecuted for righteousness' sake, For theirs is the kingdom of heaven. Blessed are you when they revile and persecute you, and say all kinds of evil against you falsely for My sake. Rejoice and be exceedingly glad, for great is your reward in heaven, for so they persecuted the prophets who were before you.

—MATTHEW 5:1–12

I enjoy good didactic sermons. Unfortunately, there are too many sermons which aren't instructive at all, but are content-less and bent on tickling emotion more than stimulating intellectual passion. My emotions are stimulated when the truth is enunciated and thus my passion is aroused to do something for God.

The greatest sermon ever preached was not preached by John Chrysostom, Charles Spurgeon, Gardner Taylor, M. L. King, Jr., H. Beecher Hicks, or T. D. Jakes. It was preached by the Son of God—Jesus Christ. The Sermon on the Mount covers Matthew 5–7. "Here is the manifesto of the new monarch, who ushers in a new age with a new message," says John MacAuthur, Jr.[2] The beatitudes, Matthew 5:1–12, could also be called the constitution of the kingdom of God. It differentiates between those who live in the kingdom and those who don't. In other words it differentiates between the saved and the unsaved.

Now, some have taught that the teaching from this sermon doesn't apply to Christians right here and now, but only in some future millennium. This is incorrect because in the millennium there won't be persecution, hunger, or sorrow!

I believe, as one Bible teacher said, that the Sermon on the Mount is relevant for the believer today. It should characterize lifestyle and practice. Jesus taught us a way of living that stemmed from a new way of thinking, which manifests a new way of life. The thrust of the Sermon on the Mount is describing how kingdom people interact between themselves and those in the world. The kingdom is an internal spiritual transformation and not an external facade. Remember, Jesus said in Luke 17:21 that "the kingdom of God is within you."

I like to refer to the Sermon on the Mount as the employee's handbook for those who are employed by the kingdom of God. Not everyone who calls Jesus "Lord" is employed by the kingdom, but only those who obey the employee's handbook!

Now, the beatitudes strongly went against the ethos of the Jewish culture of Jesus' day. You see, the last message of the Old Testament was Malachi 4:6, which says that, "He will restore the hearts of the fathers to their children and the hearts of the children to their fathers, so that [He] will not come and smite the land with a curse" (NAS). In contrast, the first sermon in the New Testament is a series of blessings called the beatitudes. The Old Testament ends with the warning of a curse; by contrast, the New Testament begins with the promise of a blessing. The Old Testament is characterized at Mount Sinai with the giving of the law amidst thunder, lighting, and judgement; in contrast, the New Testament is characterized by Mount Zion, and grace, salvation, and healing. The Old Testament demonstrates man's need of salvation; the New Testament provides the offer of a savior—Jesus Christ. The Old Testament emphasizes outward or external acts; the New Testament offers blessedness not based upon outward acts but upon new nature from within. The Old Testament is a book of the first Adam who failed miserably; the New Testament is the book of the second Adam who wonderfully succeeded.

The first Adam was tested in a beautiful garden and failed; in contrast, the last Adam was tested in a threatening wilderness and succeeded. The first Adam was a thief who was cast out of paradise; the last Adam turned to a thief on the cross and promised him paradise.

As we examine the beatitudes, I want you to take note of the pattern of how they are given. First, the principle is proclaimed, and then the promise is given. For example: "Blessed are the poor in spirit" is the principle proclaimed and "for theirs is the kingdom of heaven" is the promise given (Matt. 5:3). There are eight beatitudes:

1. Happy are the humble (verse 3)
2. Happy are the sad (verse 4)
3. Happy are the meek (verse 5)
4. Happy are the hungry (verse 6)
5. Happy are the merciful (verse 7)
6. Happy are the holy (verse 8)
7. Happy are the peacemakers (verse 9)
8. Happy are the persecuted (verses 10–12)

Now, if you read these beatitudes closely, you will discover that they are paradoxical in nature. Also, the first six (verses

3–8) are internal qualities, while the last two (verses 9–12) are outward manifestations.

The word *beatitude* stems from the very first word in each verse: *blessed*. The Greek is *makarios*, which means to be happy, fortunate, congratulations. I have defined it this way: happy and to be envied.

1. Happy are the humble (v. 3).

> Blessed are the poor in spirit, For theirs is the kingdom
> of heaven.

The word *poor* here means someone who is a beggar— remember Luke 16:20 where Lazarus is begging for food. Jesus is not advocating poverty here. More correctly, to be poor in spirit means to recognize one's spiritual poverty apart from God's grace. Apart from Jesus Christ you are spiritually bankrupt, hopeless, and helpless!

> But to this one I will look, To him who is humble and
> contrite of spirit, and who trembles at My word.
> —ISAIAH 66:2, NAS

Read the story of the Pharisee and the tax collector in Luke 18:9–14. The Pharisee was proud in spirit while the tax collector was poor in spirit.

The promise to all those who are humble in spirit is the kingdom of God.

2. Happy are the sad (v. 4).

> Blessed are those who mourn, For they shall be comforted.

Mourning is a common link to our humanity. Everyone will experience some time of mourning: perhaps the loss of a loved one, job, or a friendship. David said in Psalm 6:6–7, "I am weary with my groaning; All night I make my bed swim; I drench my couch with my tears. My eye wastes away because of grief..." You see, spiritual poverty leads to godly sorrow; the poor in spirit become those who mourn. David mourned after he sinned with Bathsheba. (See Psalm 51:3–4.) Now, happiness doesn't come in the mourning itself. The happiness comes from the forgiveness which God grants in response! You are a sinner who was saved by the grace of God. The promise to those who mourn is they shall be comforted.

The Greek word for *comfort* is *parakaleo*, which means helper, comforter, one who comes along your side to help.

Paul says in 2 Corinthians 1:3, "God of all comfort."

Robert Browning Hamilton's poem has always comforted me:

> I walked a mile with Pleasure, She chattered all the way;
> But left me none the wiser, For all she had to say.
> I walked a mile with Sorrow And ne'er a word said she;
> But, oh, the things I learned from her When Sorrow
> walked with me.[3]

3. Happy are the meek (v. 5).

> Blessed are the meek, For they shall inherit the earth.

Rome ruled the Middle East with a heavy hand. The general culture didn't encourage people to be meek because meekness was a sign of weakness. Now, the word *gentle* means mild, easygoing, or meek. Meekness doesn't mean weakness. It really is power under control. Meekness is the opposite of violence and vengeance (because a person has died to himself or herself).

"The man Moses was very meek" (Num. 12:3, kjv). The promise is they shall inherit the earth.

"The humble will inherit the land..." (Ps. 37:11, nas). It was God's intent that the meek inherit the earth.

4. Happy are the hungry (v. 6).

> Blessed are those who hunger and thirst for righteousness, for they shall be satisfied (nas).

Hunger and thirst represent the basic necessities to sustain human life on a physical level. Righteousness is also a necessity to sustain spiritual life. Without righteousness, you are starving spiritually.

> O God, You are my God; I shall seek You earnestly; My soul thirsts for You, my flesh yearns for You, In a dry and weary land where there is no water.
>
> —PSALM 63:1, NAS

My friend, what is the object of your thirst? Is it money and possessions or the kingdom of God? The promise is: when you hunger and thirst for God, He will satisfy you with the water of salvation and the bread of His Holy Spirit.

5. Happy are the merciful (v. 7).

> Blessed are the merciful, for they shall receive mercy (NAS).

Mercy was not the quality that characterized the days in which Jesus lived. The philosophers of Rome called mercy a disease of the soul and a supreme sign of weakness. The word *mercy* means to show kindness, beneficial, or charitable. Jesus showed mercy to the woman caught in the act of adultery in John 8.

I have heard some say that if you show mercy, then mercy will come back to you. But this beatitude doesn't teach that showing mercy to men will reap you mercy from men, but that mercy to men will bring mercy from God! In other words, if we are merciful to others, God will be merciful to you, whether men are merciful to you or not. I believe it's the mercy of God which brings to us:

- Forgiveness of sins
- Love unconditional
- Grace unmerited

Therefore, the promise is they shall receive mercy.

6. Happy are the holy (v. 8).

> Blessed are the pure in heart, For they shall see God.

Jesus said in Matthew 15:19–20, "For out of the heart come evil thoughts, murders, adulteries, fornications, thefts, false witness, slanders. These are the things which defile the man..." (NAS). The Greek word *katharos* means pure, clean, and undefiled from dirt, filth, and contamination. Purity of heart is more than sincerity. You see, one's motive can be sincere yet sincerely wrong. David said, "Behold, thou desirest truth in the inward parts: and in the hidden part thou shalt make me know wisdom.... Create in me a clean heart, O God; and renew a right spirit within me" (Ps. 51:6, 10, KJV). I believe that purity of heart comes by the impartation of God by His Holy Spirit. Only the pure of heart have the promise of intimate knowledge and fellowship with God.

The old hymn is true:

> This is the grand old highway our fathers all have trod,
> Walking in the highway of the King;
> The only way that leads us to heaven and to God,
> Walking in the highway of the King.
> No unclean thing can ever pass o'er this holy way
> Walking in the highway of the King.[4]

Therefore, the promise is they shall see God.

7. Happy are the peacemakers (v. 9).

> Blessed are the peacemakers, For they shall be called sons of God.

Our world desperately desires peace and harmony. But the reality is our world is filled with violence and brokenness. This beatitude calls upon God's people to be peacemakers and reconcilers.

> Pursue peace with all *people*, and holiness, without which no one will see the Lord.
>
> —HEBREWS 12:14

Peace cannot come where sin and injustice prevail.

> Mercy and truth have met together; Righteousness and peace have kissed.
>
> —PSALM 85:10

Jesus made it clear that He came not to bring peace but to bring a sword. In other words, when God's righteousness is upheld, it will create strife and opposition. The Father is the source of peace, the Son is the manifestation of that peace, and the Holy Spirit is the agent of that peace. The promise is that peacemakers shall be called sons of God.

8. Happy are the persecuted (vs. 10–12).

This last beatitude is really two in one. "Blessed" is mentioned twice but is connected as a single thought by the word *persecuted.*

The persecuted

> Indeed, all who desire to live godly in Christ Jesus will be persecuted.
>
> —2 TIMOTHY 3:12, NAS

To live for Christ will bring you opposition from Satan. Persecution is not incidental to faithful Christian living but is certain evidence of it. This is normal Christianity!

The promise is that theirs is the kingdom (v. 10).

- Physical persecution: "Blessed are those who are persecuted for righteousness' sake" (v.10).

- Verbal insults: "Blessed are you when they revile and persecute you"; cast insults against you (v. 11).

- False accusation: "Say all kinds of evil against you falsely for My sake" (v. 11).

The posture: "Rejoice and be exceedingly glad" (v. 12). Why?

- "...for great *is* your reward in heaven..."

- "...for so they persecuted the prophets who were before you."

My friend, you'll never be able to fulfill the beatitudes with just the shear force of your will, but only by the indwelling of the Holy Spirit. Once again, I believe the beatitudes are the employee's handbook of those employed by the King of the kingdom.

Finally, some folks don't have a positive beatitude, they just parade an attitude. With great humor, mixed with great insight, Patsy Clairmont has observed several types of "tudes":[5]

- Negative—tude
- Nasty—tude
- Fussy—tude
- Fighting—tude
- Backbiting—tude
- Uncooperative—tude
- Deceitful—tude
- Lying—tude
- Ingratitude
- Envy—tude
- Jealous—tude
- Loveless—tude
- Gossip—tude
- Cranky—tude

But the beatitudes teach us to have an attitude of gratitude. I like to call it a love-tude! A love-tude is very optimistic and positive, no matter the circumstances or situation. Let me illustrate it with the following story:

Ted and Mike were paid to search for wolves in the Midwestern United States. After weeks of searching, they found no wolves and were thinking about giving up. But one day, after another exhausting search, they laid down to rest. Ted nudged Mike in the middle of the night to inform him that the two hunters were surrounded by twenty-five snarling wolves! Mike said to Ted, "Brother, we're rich." You see it's really all about one's attitude toward adversity that will determine success or failure in life. Let's cultivate, with help from God, a positive beatitude.

Chapter 3

LOVE ONE ANOTHER

———◆◆◆———

When I invited Jesus into my life, I thought He was going to put up some wallpaper and hang a few pictures. But He started knocking out walls and adding on rooms. I said, 'I was expecting a nice cottage.' But He said, 'I'm making a palace in which to live.'"[1]

—C. S. Lewis

So, when he had gone out, Jesus said, "Now the Son of Man is glorified, and God is glorified in Him. If God is glorified in Him, God will also glorify Him in Himself, and glorify Him immediately. Little children, I shall be with you a little while longer. You will seek Me; and as I said to the Jews, 'Where I am going, you cannot come,' so now I say to you. A new commandment I give to you, that you love one another; as I have loved you, that you also love one another. By this all will know that you are My disciples, if you have love for one another."

—John 13:31-35

The last week of Jesus' life was filled with stress and anxiety. He knew that His hour was about to come. It was six days before He would celebrate Passover in the upper room in Jerusalem. Caiaphas, who was elected high priest that year, was conservative and comfortable with the arrangement he worked out with Rome. He called a surprise meeting. Jesus was attracting the attention of Rome. If He wasn't stopped, the religious establishment would lose their place in the hearts of the people and Rome might invade the nation. "Jesus must die to save the nation," said Caiaphas. Lazarus must also die. A few days later, Jesus rode a donkey into Jerusalem with great fanfare in a parade. The people treated Him as a king; as the long-awaited Messiah.

Later in the day He had a private moment with His followers. He dropped a bombshell on them, telling them that He would only be with them for a short while. About a day before Passover, on Thursday, He and the disciples were eating when He did something unusual; He took a towel and began to wash their feet. Afterwards He dropped another bombshell upon His disciples when He said, "one of you will betray me" (Matt. 26:21). Then Satan entered Judas, and as he was about to get up Jesus told him, "What you do, do quickly" (John 13:27). The rest of the disciples thought Judas was going to get some more food. The disciples began arguing about who was going to be the boss when Jesus establishes His kingdom.

What I've just described is the context in which our text is located. The strain and stress of it all must have been unbearable for Jesus. So, in the midst of hell bearing down upon Him and the knowledge He was going to be betrayed by Judas; denied by Peter, and the disciples; scourged and tortured by the Roman guards; and forsaken by His father, Jesus uttered words which have literally changed the world forever—"Love one another." How can He amidst great adversity make such a statement? How can He, while even being crucified, say "Father, forgive them; for they know not what they do" (Luke 23:34, KJV)? I submit to you He could endure the agonizing, excruciating pain of crucifixion and godforsakenness because He placed a higher value on obedience to the Father's will.

He would say it this way: "If you love Me, keep My commandments" (John 14:15).

Or He would say, "He who has My commandments and keeps them, it is he who loves me. And he who loves Me will be loved by My Father" (John 14:21).

Or: "You are My friends if you do whatever I command you" (John 15:14).

You see if you're going to be a follower of Jesus you must obey and follow His commands. The hymn says: "Trust and obey, trust and obey, the only way to live happy in Jesus is if you trust and obey."[2] This accurately states what getting over ourselves in order to live a purposeful kingdom life is all about.

He said, "Love one another!"

Now, returning to our text for a moment (John 13:31–32), Jesus will glorify His Father and Himself. He says the same thing in John 12:23: "The hour has come for the Son of Man to be glorified" (NAS). He also says, "Father, glorify Your name" (John 12:28, NAS). And in John 17:1–5, Jesus prays that the Father would glorify Him with the glory He had before the worlds were formed.

So what is this business of being glorified? The Greek word *doxa* means to have a high opinion of someone; to have a good reputation; to speak well of someone. It came to mean splendor, radiance, and majesty of God.

What is your opinion of Jesus? Do you see Him as splendid, radiant, and altogether lovely? You must give God the glory.

In verse 33, Jesus says He will be with His disciples in the flesh for a little while longer. He now calls the disciples "little children." The apostle John uses this phrase all the time in his epistles. It means one who is dependent upon another for support. Jesus said unless you becomes like a little child you cannot be His disciple, because the kingdom of God belongs to the children. (See Matthew 18:4; Mark 10:15; Luke 18:17.) Are you a child dependent upon God, your Father, or are you an independent adult relying upon your own strength?

In verses 34–35, Jesus issues a new commandment: love one another. Take note that Christ emphasizes He is the one issuing this commandment. The emphasis here is that this command is not by some intermediary or middleman but is directly from His mouth. His intent is that you're hearing this directly from Me so that you won't mess it up. Now, in the Bible, only two people could issue a command: a king or God. A command is basically a law, edict, or statute. Jesus said a "new" commandment. There are two words in the Greek for *new*. The Greek word *kainos* means fresh, unused; for example, a new car. But the other word *neos* means new in kind; never seen before. For example, if a primitive person were to see a car, it would be radically new to him!

This "new" commandment isn't in the sense that it has never been around before. TV advertisements call a product new and improved though the product has been around for a while. Jesus is saying that love has always been God's intent:

- "You shall love your neighbor as yourself" (Lev. 19:18).

- "You shall love your neighbor as yourself" (Matt. 19:19).

The newness of the command is not love, but to "love one another; as I have loved you" (v. 34). Therefore, the new commandment is to love one another as Christ loved us.

This new commandment has three aspects to it:

1. Love one another

The phrase is used seven times in the New Testament: John 13:34, 15:17; 1 Thessalonians 4:9; 1 John 3:11, 23; 4:7, 21.

I submit to you that not only are we to love one another, but the Bible says:

- "Bearing with one another in love" (Eph. 4:2).

- "We are members of one another" (Eph. 4:25).

- "Be kind to one another" (Eph. 4:32).

- "Do not lie to one another" (Col. 3:9).

- "... admonishing one another in psalms" (Col. 3:16).

- "Abound in love to one another" (1 Thess. 3:12).

- "Comfort one another" (1 Thess. 4:18).

- "Edify one another" (1 Thess. 5:11).

- "Do not speak evil of one another" (James 4:11).

How are we to love one another?

2. Jesus said, "Love one another; as I have loved you" (John 13:34).

How did Jesus show His love for us? He sacrificially laid His life down for us. Jesus is establishing the principle of sacrificial love. How can we love sacrificially?

- Showing kindness to others

- Showing patience to others

- Showing genuine concern for others

- Serving others

- Laying down your life for others

It's going to cost you to love another. Every mother knows this principle. Every parent who has a disabled child knows this principle. I declare unto you that this is what Jesus meant when He said: "Love one another; as I have loved you, that you also love one another."

Allow me to illustrate this point. During the Korean War, a U.S. soldier was shocked to uncover a live baby underneath a woman who was frozen to death. The mother had taken her jacket off, wrapped it around the baby, then wrapped herself around the baby—she froze to death, but the baby was found alive.

Jesus took you, wrapped you in Him, and sheltered you from the cold. He died so that you may live.

3. "By this all will know that you are My disciples, if you have love for one another" (John 13:35).

There is no evangelistic program that can produce greater fruit than brothers or sisters loving one another. The world will know that we are Christ's disciples, not by our programs or committees, not by our beautiful sanctuary, but by our love for one another.

A disciple is one who follows, or is a learner of another person. The disciple gradually becomes like his teacher.

It ought to be that the more you are around Jesus the more you look like Him, talk like Him, and act like Him. This question is: are you becoming more loving as a person towards others or less loving? Our world is filled with tension, conflict, strife, and hatred. Jesus' challenge to us is that when we love one another "all will know" that we are Christ's. But if we mirror the world, we negate the message of Jesus Christ and disobey His direct command.

> Jesus, Lord, we look to Thee;
> Let us in Thy Name agree;
> Show Thyself the Prince of Peace,
> Bid our strife forever cease.
>
> Make us of one heart and mind,
> Gentle, courteous, and kind,
> Lowly, meek, in thought and word,
> Altogether like our Lord.
>
> Free from anger and from pride;
> Let us thus in God abide;
> All the depths of love express,
> All the heights of holiness.[3]

My friends, we need to know that...

- Love can take you where you need to go,

- Love can take your test-a-many and give you a testimony,

- Love can take you from the pit of despair to the rock of hope,

- Love can turn your enemies into your closest friends,

- Love can turn that cantankerous man into a charming Denzel Washington,

- Love can turn that obstinate woman into the most beautiful woman, who would be the envy of all,

- Love is what makes a house a home,

- Love is what makes a functional family out of a dysfunctional one.

I tell you love is what we need, not religion or more committees! Jesus came to our address and said I love you enough to die for you, and I only have one request: love your brothers and sisters in the way that I have loved you. I tell you that Jesus loves you always.

He said in Matthew 28:20, "Lo, I am with you always, even to the end of the age." When we practice loving one another sacrificially as Christ loved us, then we will have obeyed the new commandment. John 15:13 says: "Greater love has no one than this, than to lay down one's life for his friends." It is this selfless act of loving one another that helps us learn how to get over ourselves. This is something we must be taught to do. This point is beautifully illustrated by Orla C. Shup Albion:[4]

> When I baby-sit for my minister's three-year-old, one of our favorite games is Go Fish. One evening, after winning several rounds, she kept bragging about how good she was. Jokingly, I said to her, "I'm going to have to teach you a little humility." Immediately she looked up and asked, "How do you play that?"

Chapter 4

GET OVER YOURSELF

—⸱◈⸱—

When Christ calls a man, He bids him come and die.[1]
—DIETRICH BONHOEFFER

Therefore if there is any consolation in Christ, if any comfort of love, if any fellowship of the Spirit, if any affection and mercy, fulfill my joy by being like-minded, having the same love, being of one accord, of one mind.
—PHILIPPIANS 2:1 (SEE ALSO PHIL. 2:2–10)

The state of relationships, be they marriage, friendship, parental, or coworker is in trouble today. Relationships are more difficult to develop and harder to maintain. The evidence of this is all around us, for example:

- Marriages are falling apart at an alarming rate, now over 50 percent.

- Friendships don't last as long anymore.

- The work environment is filled with tension, strife, and acrimony.

There is no longer the commitment to work at establishing or maintaining relationships; there exists today a "try and see" attitude.

How many of you have kept in contact with your best friend from grade school? High school? Or college? We lose contact with friends over the years.

Yet, despite the fact that relationships are in trouble, we continue to strive to be in a relationship. Just look at the explosion of dating and relationship services. In fact, some people advertise in the newspaper their desire to meet someone! What is my take on all this? I think the number one problem in relationships is that fundamentally the individuals involved are often selfish, self-centered, and self-sufficient. Their attitude toward the other person in the relationship is, *Move over*. This is because they have built their own kingdom and are unaware of the kingdom of God. They are innately preoccupied with the way they appear, how they dress, how they think, what they desire, and what they crave. It is really all about *me*! It is this philosophy: I am the center of my world; and such a view is what hinders relationships.

Our lives are unequivocally sharpened by our relationships. In some respects we are the product of the relationships we've experienced over the years. Some of those relationships have been constructive and positive, other relationships have been destructive and negative. Too many of our relationships are toxic. And it is the toxicity of such relationships that kills you, just as taking poison. I believe you should evaluate your relationships, because as seasons come and go, so do relationships.

- Why is this person in my life?

- Are they here to do me good or harm?

- Do I feel encouraged or discouraged after being around them?

- Do they challenge me to be a better person?

People will come in and out of your life for a reason, find out why they are in your life. Also, in relationships you need to distinguish between primary and secondary ones.

Primary relationships

- Nurturing, affirming, supportive, intimate, and informal

- Crucial for emotional and psychological stability, e.g. mother, father, and close friends

Secondary relationships

- Casual, formal, and not intimate, e.g. coworkers, neighbors, and mailpeople

One other thing: God created human beings to be social and interactive, not aloof and inactive. We were made for community and social interaction. The English poet John Donne expressed it well: "No man is an island entirely unto himself, but each man is a part of a continent apart of a whole."

Perhaps there is no other teaching that most powerfully states the secret to having fulfilling relationships than the Golden Rule:

> So in everything, do to others what you would have them do to you, for this sums up the Law and the Prophets.
>
> —MATTHEW 7:12, NIV

> And just as you want men to do to you, you also do to them likewise.
>
> —LUKE 6:31

I have always believed that the key to experiencing fulfilling relationships is treating others with respect, honor, and dignity, because this is how I want to be treated. The story of Jacob is a good example of the old saying, "What goes around, comes around." He deceived his brother Esau and his father Isaac only to be deceived by his Uncle Laban.

I think there is something else which is a hindrance to fulfilling relationships. It is that we are disconnected from one another by the walls we erect. Some have erected walls to protect themselves from being disappointed, abused emotionally, or hurt psychologically. So we become like Humpty Dumpty. I am sure you remember the children's nursery rhyme. Well, there are many people who sit atop walls that they have erected to protect themselves emotionally. But these walls only cause them to fall down like Humpty! One of the secrets to fulfilling relationships is to stop erecting walls and start connecting with people.

In his excellent book *Connecting*, Dr. Larry Crabb says, "When two people connect, when their beings intersect … something is poured out of one and into the other that has the power to heal the soul of its deepest wounds and restore it to health."[2] The secret is within our connecting with one another as we struggle together to make each other whole. So, "I need you and you need me," that's the way God made it to be. But you will never connect until you get over yourself.

Now what does Philippians 2:1–11 have to do with any of this? Everything! Our text is an admonition from the apostle Paul for humility. This is the key for me in order to reject my self-built kingdom and to embrace the kingdom of God. His point is that if you can get over yourself by humbling yourself like Jesus Christ, you will experience a satisfying relationship with God and with others. Philippians is perhaps the apostle Paul's most upbeat letter. He is genuinely happy. But his happiness is not based upon his outward circumstances. It is based upon an inward resolve about his relationship with Jesus Christ. His circumstances were arduous and hard:

- He was in prison.

- He was physically tired … since his conversion he spent twenty years of missionary travels and preaching the gospel of Jesus. (See Philippians 1:21–26.)

- His ministry was effective, but some within the church didn't like it. They were jealous and started competing with Paul. (See Philippians 1:14–18.)

In Philippians 2:1–11, the apostle Paul says two important things:

1. Become humble … why? (vv. 1–4)

2. Because this is what Jesus Christ did (vv. 5–11). Observe the conditional conjunction "if" used in verse one:

> Therefore *if* there is any consolation [encouragement]
> in Christ, *if* any comfort of love, *if* any fellowship of the
> Spirit, *if* any affection [tenderness] and mercy [compas-
> sion]...
>
> —PHILIPPIANS 2:1 (EMPHASIS ADDED)

Now, because you have encouragement, comfort, fellowship, affection, and mercy within Christ, Paul says take your
focus off yourself and put it upon your brothers and sisters.
In other words, get over yourself and learn to become "like-
minded." How am I to achieve this?

- Have the same love

- Be of one accord

- Do nothing out of selfish ambition or conceit

- Humble yourself and esteem the other person
  (honor/respect) more than you do yourself

- Don't just be concerned with your own interests, but
  seek to understand the interests of others.

I firmly believe that the secret to getting over you is to
humble yourself and come under the kingdom rule of Jesus
Christ.

In verses 5–11, the apostle Paul uses Jesus Christ as illustration. Christ humbles Himself by taking upon the form of
a servant. (See John 13:3–17 where Jesus washes the feet of
the disciples.) But the remarkable thing about the humility
of Christ is that God has exalted Him. So, here's the point of
this message: you will only experience fulfilling relationships
to the degree that you, like Christ, humble yourself. In other
words, get over yourself. I believe many relationships would be
better if we would humble ourselves.

Dr. Kevin Leman, in his fine book *Winning the Rat Race
without Becoming a Rat,* gives this excellent illustration: When
Mike Lorelli was a top-dog at Pizza Hut, one of his favorite

people was Mary, the cleaning woman. He would stop and talk to her and spend as much time with her as anybody else he would bump into in the hallways of Pizza Hut's corporate offices. Later, as life often turns out, he learned that Mary's brother was the same person who does his lawn and yard work. One day Mary's brother stopped him and said, "Mr. Lorelli, you're one of my favorite people in the world because you give time to my sister, Mary, who cleans in your building. I think this is getting right down to why you are the way you are and what has really made you successful in business. An attitude that is willing to spend time with Mary is an attitude that will reach out and enfold everyone."[3] So, in conclusion, get over yourself and take time to relate to people without some selfish motive. And how do you address your innate selfish motives? By humbling yourself and voluntarily coming under the kingdom rule of Jesus Christ. I believe, in the end, this is the best formula for experiencing satisfying relationships.

Chapter 5

I LOVE YOU AND THERE'S NOTHING YOU CAN DO ABOUT IT

⟫⟪

The central sin is the sin of trying to make yourself God. The word "evil" is the word "live" spelled backwards. It is an attempt to live life against itself. Self-surrender is more of an offer than a demand.[1]

—STANLEY JONES

But when the Pharisees heard that He had silenced the Sadducees, they gathered together. Then one of them, a lawyer, asked Him a question, testing Him, and saying, "Teacher, which is the great commandment in the law?" Jesus said to him, "You shall love the LORD your God with all your heart, with all your soul, and with all your mind. This is the first and great commandment. And the second is like it: 'You shall love your neighbor as yourself.' On these two commandments hang all the Law and the Prophets."

—MATTHEW 22:34–40

At Faith Tabernacle, there's a practice we have that's been somewhat of a trademark. When we greet visitors, while facing one another, we will say, "I love you and there's nothing you can do about it." People really need to know that they are loved.

We hear a lot about love today. We are told we ought to love people and treat them in a certain way. But, there are hate groups, such as the Klan or Nazi skinheads, who preach a gospel of hate and separation. Also, families seem to be breaking up at an alarming rate. The love of husbands and wives seem to grow dimmer as the years pass by.

Today, we seem more comfortable with being alone and

aloof than together, joined in community. We have all types of communication devices–cell phones, e-mail, etc.–but we really communicate less today than at any other time in history.

Though we try to isolate ourselves, the reality is God was right when He said, "It is not good that man should be alone" (Gen. 2:18). We are created to be social, and not to be islands. Again, the poet John Donne was correct when he wrote: "No man is an island entire to himself; every man is a piece of a whole."

The challenge we face today as Christians is whether or not we will obey the law of love within a cultural context that has as its national anthem the Tina Turner song, "What's Love Got to Do with It?"

If we're not careful, we can grow cold and calloused toward one another and love will die. Revelation 2:4 says that the church of Ephesus allowed its love to grow weak: "You have left your first love." This was its love for Christ and for one another.

I wonder if you can identify with this: Lucy and Snoopy were talking together in Charles Schultz's familiar comic strip "Peanuts." She shouts, "There are times when you really bug me! I must admit, however, there are times when I feel like giving you a hug." In a nonchalant manner Snoopy responds, "That's the way I am, Lucy, huggable and buggable!"[2] So, this illustrates my point when I say I love you and there is nothing you can do about it, including people who are huggable and buggable!

Now, our text is within the context of Jesus having been confronted by the religious leaders of His day who were jealous of Him.

- The Pharisees asked Him if it is lawful to pay taxes to the government (Matt. 22:15–21).

- The Sadducees asked Him about the resurrection (Matt. 22:23–33).

- A lawyer asked Him what the greatest commandment is (Matt. 22:34–40).

Jesus' response:

- Love God with all your heart, soul, and mind (entirely with everything within you) and...

- Love your neighbor as yourself. (See Matthew 22:37–39). Our Lord is quoting Deuteronomy 6:4–5—the Hebrew *Shema* and Leviticus 19:12.

Now, there are three primary Greek words for our English word *love*:

- *Eros* means erotic/sexual

- *Philo* means close friends

- *Agape* means unconditional/unmerited

The law of love is one's unconditional acceptance of another. It is you being prepared to lay down your personal agenda to seek another's highest good. In point of fact, it is self surrender. Listen to the following references on this point:

- "For God so loved the world..." (John 3:16).

- "Husbands, love your wives, just as Christ also loved the church" (Eph. 5:25).

- "By this we know love, because He laid down His life for us" (1 John 3:16).

No doubt, the clearest expression of this law of love is found in Paul's comments in 1 Corinthians 13.

Now, how do you know if you really love God? Is it predicated on some emotional feeling? Or something deeper? Listen to the words of Jesus:

- "For this is the love of God, that we keep His commandments. And His commandments are not burdensome" (1 John 5:3).

- "If you love Me, keep My commandments" (John 14:15).

- "He who has My commandments and keeps them, it is he who loves Me" (John 14:21).

- "If anyone loves Me, he will keep My word" (John 14:23).

So, what commandments did Jesus leave for us? (See John 13:34–35 and John 15:12.)

What's new about the commandment to love? The phrase: "That you love one another; as I have loved you" (John 13:34). What is the scope of the law of love? Jesus taught in Matthew 5:44: "Love your enemies." Paul added clarification of how to do this in Romans 12:20: "If your enemy is hungry, feed him; If he is thirsty, give him a drink; For in so doing you will heap coals of fire on his head." Also, James 5:20 states that love will "cover a multitude of sins."

A Biblical illustration of the law of love is the prophet Hosea:

> When the Lord began to speak by Hosea, the Lord said to Hosea: "Go, take yourself a wife of harlotry And children of harlotry, For the land has committed great harlotry By departing from the LORD."
>
> —HOSEA 1:2

Hosea marries a prostitute named Gomer, and they have three children:

1. Jezreel means "God scatters." (See Hosea 1:4.)

2. Lo-Ruhaman means "no mercy." (See Hosea 1:6.)

3. Lo-Ammi means "not my people." (See Hosea 1:9.)

> I will betroth you to Me forever, Yes, I will betroth you to Me In righteousness and justice, In lovingkindness and mercy.
>
> —HOSEA 2:19

We hear a lot about love today. I believe it's time to allow God's love to capture our hearts so we can manifest it one to another. This is the quality that indicates whether you're a kingdom person or not. You can search the pages of Holy Scripture and you will discover that:

James 2:8 calls it "the royal law."

1 John 3:1 says, "Behold what manner of love the Father has bestowed on us, that we should be called the children of God!"

1 John 4:7 says, "Beloved, let us love one another, for love is of God; and everyone who loves is born of God and knows God."

1 John 4:16 says, "God is love."

1 John 4:19 says, "We love Him because He first loved us."

Paul said in Romans 5:8 "But God demonstrates His own love toward us, in that while we were still sinners, Christ died for us."

2 Corinthians 5:14 says, "For the love of Christ compels us, because we judge thus: that if One died for all, then all died."

It is with this understanding of the law of love that Philip P. Bliss wrote:

> I am so glad that our Father in heaven
> Tells of love in the book He has given,
> Wonderful things in the Bible I see.
> This the dearest, that Jesus loves me.
> I am so glad that Jesus loves me, even me.[3]

We all know that famous children's song that says, "Jesus loves me this I know. For the Bible tells me so." And we probably all know the great hymn of the church "Love Lifted Me":[4]

> I was sinking deep in sin, far from the peaceful shore,
> Very deeply stained within, sinking to rise no more;
> But the master of the sea heard my despairing cry,
> From the waters lifted me—now safe am I.
> Love lifted me, love lifted me,
> When nothing else could help,
> Love, lifted me.

I think the law of love is very crucial in understanding how to get over yourself. This is primarily because the fundamental nature of love focuses its attention away from self and toward the other person.

Finally, what is the greatest commandment? It is to love God with heart, soul, and mind, and to love your neighbor as yourself. By doing this, you prove you're a kingdom person. In the magazine *Peacemaking Day by Day*, Mother Teresa was profoundly correct when she said:

> I have come more and more to realize that being unwanted is the worst disease that any human being can ever experience. Nowadays we have found medicine for leprosy, and lepers can be cured. There's medicine for TB, and consumption can be cured. But for being unwanted, except there are willing hands to serve and there's a loving heart to love, I don't think this terrible disease can be cured.[5]

When you look a person in the eyes and say to them, "I love you and there's nothing you can do about it," what you're really saying is: "I am learning how to live as a citizen of the kingdom because I am learning to get over myself so that I can get involved with you."

Chapter 6

NO TIME FOR FAULTFINDING

He who learns must suffer. And even in our sleep pain that cannot forget falls drop by drop upon the heart, and in our own despair, against our will, comes wisdom to us by the awful grace of God.[1]

—AESCHYLUS

Judge not, that you be not judged. For with what judgment you judge, you will be judged; and with the measure you use, it will be measured back to you. And why do you look at the speck in your brother's eye, but do not consider the plank in your own eye? Or how can you say to your brother, "Let me remove the speck out of your eye"; and look, a plank is in your own eye? Hypocrite! First remove the plank from your own eye, and then you will see clearly to remove the speck from your brother's eye.

—MATTHEW 7:1–5

Therefore be merciful, just as your Father also is merciful. Judge not, and you shall not be judged. Condemn not, and you shall not be condemned. Forgive, and you will be forgiven.

—LUKE 6:36–37

It is a fact that we judge people by what they do and ourselves by our good intentions.

Some have interpreted these verses to mean that Jesus forbids evaluation, honest difference of opinion, or honest criticism. Such a view is wrong. Are we not to say anything about a brother or sister who sins or is morally corrupt? Of course not! What Jesus is addressing is the spirit of judgment, faultfinding, and nit-picking, which is so common among church folk.

You see, the Pharisees with their good intentions established their own rules and traditions. The Pharisees had set up such a standard that no one could measure up. Now, these Pharisees were mean-spirited, negative, critical, and divisive. Really, these Pharisees were hypocrites who didn't even measure up to their own rules. Their organizational anthem was: "Do as I say and overlook what I do." When you give in to a judgmental and critical spirit, you are in trouble; what if our heavenly Father adopted this attitude? Psalm 130:3–4 says, "If You, LORD, should mark iniquities [take notes], O Lord, who could stand? But there is forgiveness with You, That You may be feared."

In our text I want you to notice four principles. My thoughts about this text have been greatly influenced by the exegesis of Dr. John McAurther. I recommend to all the MacArthur New Testament commentaries.[2]

1. An erroneous view of God (Matt. 7:1)

Judgmentalism is wrong because it manifests a wrong view of God.

Observe the phrase in Matthew 7:1: "that you be not judged." Jesus reminds the Pharisees and us as well, that we are not the final court of judgment. To judge another person's motives or to condemn is really to play God.

- Who are you to judge another? (Romans 14:4)
- There is only one lawgiver and judge (James 4:11–12).

I don't believe Jesus is saying to cease examining and discerning, but to cease being judgmental and critical.

2. An erroneous view of others (Matt. 7:2)

Judgmentalism is wrong because it manifests an erroneous view of others.

We believe we are free to judge others because of our pride and sense of superiority. All the while we are not realizing that the manner in which you judge others will be the manner in which you are judged. When you judge, the law of sowing and reaping takes effect. Eugene Peterson, in *The Message*, says, "That critical spirit has a way of boomeranging."[3]

- Observe the Pharisee's prideful prayer versus the tax gatherer's humble prayer in Luke 18:11–14.

- "God shows personal favoritism to no man" (Gal. 2:6).

3. An erroneous view of ourselves (Matthew 3–4)

Judgmentalism is wrong because it manifests an erroneous view of ourselves.

If you have a wrong view of God then you'll have a wrong view of others and of yourself. Hence, we look at the *speck* in someone else, which is a real area of sin in the person's life, but, we forget the *log* in our own lives, which may be a larger sin than that of our brother or sister. This is the problem of self-righteousness.

4. The right balance (Matthew 7:5)

The word *hypocrite* means to play act. In Greek dramas the actors on stage would wear different masks. Jesus' point here is first to take off your mask. Deal with yourself first before you judge someone else.

I believe that a major problem in the church is the critical and judgmental spirit which has deceived so many. We are so judgmental, nitpicky, and self-righteous that I can hear God say "enough is enough."

My friend, don't talk about how "such and such ain't doing this or that," if you ain't doing nothing either! Furthermore, don't talk about any auxiliary or ministry of your church if you aren't willing to lend it a helping hand! At the risk of being blunt: if you don't have anything positive to say, then keep your mouth shut and just pray for the person or situation! If you persist in your pharisaical, self-righteous judgments, then God will judge you the way you have judged others. Please, just get over yourself!

I wish some church folk would adopt this philosophy regarding faultfinding and judgmentalism: "When it comes to thinking about anything but Jesus, I just don't have the time." I wish some church folk would spend more time thinking about Jesus than about another brother or sister. I wish they would adapt the attitude that says, "I don't have time to gossip or murmur because Jesus occupies too much of my thinking! I don't have time to judge or be critical because I'm too busy praising God! I don't have time to sit around and say, 'Aw the church ain't this or that,' because I am too busy thinking about the goodness of Jesus and all He's done for me!"

At the heart of faultfinding is an exalted view of myself and consequently a lower view of my brother or sister. We must learn how to get over ourselves if we are going to live purposeful lives for the kingdom of God. Dr. Martin Luther King, Jr. once said: "Every man must decide whether he will walk in the light of creative altruism or the darkness of destructive selfishness. This is the judgment. Life's most persistent and urgent question is: what are you doing for others?"[4] There is no more time for faultfinding.

Recently, a member of the church where I pastor passed on to me this story which I think illustrates my point:

Ruth went to her mailbox and there was only one letter. She picked it up and looked at it before opening, but then she looked at the envelope again. There was no stamp, no postmark, only her name and address. She read the letter:

> Dear Ruth:
> I'm going to be in your neighborhood Saturday afternoon and I'd like to stop by for a visit.
>
> Love Always, Jesus

Her hands were shaking as she placed the letter on the table. "Why would the Lord want to visit me? I'm nobody special. I don't have anything to offer." With that thought, Ruth remembered her empty kitchen cabinets. "Oh my goodness, I really don't have anything to offer. I'll have to run down to the store and buy something for dinner." She reached for her purse and counted out its contents: five dollars and forty cents. "Well, I can get some bread and cold cuts, at least." She threw on her coat and hurried out the door. A loaf of French bread, a half-pound of sliced turkey, and a carton of milk ... leaving Ruth with a grand total of twelve cents to last her until Monday. Nonetheless, she felt good as she headed home, her meager offerings tucked under her arm.

"Hey lady, can you help us, lady?" Ruth had been so absorbed in her dinner plans she hadn't even noticed two figures huddled in the alleyway. A man and a woman, both of them dressed in little more than rags.

"Look lady, I ain't got a job, ya know, and my wife and I have been living out here on the street, and, well, now it's getting cold and we're getting kinda hungry and, well, if you could help us, lady, we'd really appreciate it."

Ruth looked at them both. They were dirty, they smelled bad, and frankly she was certain that they could get some kind of work if they really wanted to.

"Sir, I'd like to help you, but I'm a poor woman myself. All I have is a few cold cuts and some bread, and I'm having an important guest for dinner tonight. I was planning on serving that to Him."

"Yeah, well, okay lady, I understand. Thanks anyway."

The man put his arm around the woman's shoulders, turned, and headed back into the alley. As she watched them leave, Ruth felt a familiar twinge in her heart. "Sir, wait!" The couple stopped and turned as she ran down the alley after them. "Look, why don't you take this food. I'll figure out something else to serve my guest." She handed the man her grocery bag. "Thank you lady. Thank you very much!"

"Yes, thank you!" said the man's wife, and Ruth could see now that she was shivering. "You know, I've got another coat at home. Here, why don't you take this one." Ruth unbuttoned her jacket and slipped it over the woman's shoulders. Then, smiling she turned and walked back to the street ... without her coat and with nothing to serve her guest. "Thank you lady! Thank you very much!"

Ruth was chilled by the time she reached her front door, and worried too. The Lord was coming to visit and she didn't have anything to offer Him. She fumbled through her purse for the door key. But as she did, she noticed another envelope in her mailbox. "That's odd. The mailman doesn't usually come twice in one day." She took the envelope out of the box and opened it.

Dear Ruth:
It was so good to see you again. Thank you for the lovely meal. And thank you, too, for the beautiful coat.

Love Always, Jesus

The air was still cold, but even without her coat Ruth no longer noticed.

Chapter 7

YOU MUST BE BORN "OVER AGAIN"

———⟫•⟪———

The man who knows his sins is greater than one who raises a dead man by his prayers. He who sighs and grieves within himself for an hour is greater than one who teaches the entire universe. He who follows Christ, alone and contrite, is greater than one who enjoys the favor of the crowds in the churches.[1]

—St. Isaac, The Syrian

There was a man of the Pharisees named Nicodemus, a ruler of the Jews. This man came to Jesus by night and said to Him, "Rabbi, we know that You are a teacher come from God; for no one can do these signs that You do unless God is with him." Jesus answered and said to him, "Most assuredly, I say to you, unless one is born again, he cannot see the kingdom of God." Nicodemus said to Him, "How can a man be born when he is old? Can he enter a second time into his mother's womb and be born?" Jesus answered, "Most assuredly, I say to you, unless one is born of water and the Spirit, he cannot enter the kingdom of God. That which is born of the flesh is flesh, and that which is born of the Spirit is spirit. Do not marvel that I said to you, 'You must be born again.' The wind blows where it wishes, and you hear the sound of it, but cannot tell where it comes from and where it goes. So is everyone who is born of the Spirit." Nicodemus answered and said to him, "How can these things be?" Jesus answered and said to him, "Are you the teacher of Israel, and do not know these things? Most assuredly, I say to you, We speak what We know and testify what We have seen, and you do not receive Our witness. If I have told you earthly things and you do not believe, how will you believe if I tell you heavenly things?"

—JOHN 3:1–12

The birth of a baby is an amazing event. The delivery process is both exhilarating and exhausting. Family, friends, and neighbors all get excited and "pumped up" when they hear that a new baby is about to be born. I ask you, what's more exciting than the birth of a baby? I was in the delivery room when my son was born and I coached Debbie on how to breathe (my Lamaze training) and push. It was amazing. Have you ever thought about the fact that God allows us the privilege of cooperating with Him in the process of creating life? However, no human birth can compare to the rejoicing "by the angels in heaven" when one sinner is born over again by the Spirit. You see, spiritual birth is eternal, whereas natural birth is temporary.

When God created mankind, according to Genesis 1:26, humankind was created in the moral image of God. It was God's intent that:

- Humankind live forever

- Humankind enjoy relationship with Him

- Humankind rule the earth and exercise dominion

- Humankind was to be fruitful and multiply; populate the earth.

But in Genesis chapter three, the decision Adam made to disobey God (perhaps the worst event in human history) led him to fall. God warned Adam and Eve that the day they ate of the forbidden fruit they would die. Adam lived nine hundred thirty years physically, but he died spiritually on the day he chose to disobey. His decision had disastrous consequences for humankind, such as:

- Lost relationship with God
- Lost relationship with one another

- Lost rulership/dominion

Now, when Jesus arrived on the earthly scene as the second Adam, He restored through His sacrifice our *rulership* and *relationship* with God. Two words, "restoration" and "transformation," characterized Jesus' ministry. To experience this new birth, Jesus said you must be born over again.

My friend, because of your sins you are spiritually dead, though you are alive physically. It is like a tall tree that looks healthy, but once a strong wing blows it falls down because it is hollow. John Wesley said, "This then is why new birth is required. Our entire nature has become corrupted. It is precisely because we have been born into a sinful world that we now must be 'born again.'"[2]

I believe that one of the most profound truths in all of Christian theology, dogma, and creeds is this notion that one can be born over again. The new birth is the first step in the process of salvation. Think about it, God offers to rebellious, cantankerous, hardheaded, mean-spirited folks like you and me another chance!

On May 10, 1999, a *Washington Times* article entitled "Unconscious America" stated that Americans are in a crisis of conscience. In a national poll, fifty-six percent surveyed said the major problems in America aren't the economy, environment, or education, but moral decline and decay.[3]

I believe more laws or throwing money at problems won't solve the moral and ethical demise that is occurring in America. Our only hope is the gospel, which says, "You must be born over again!" In other words, people need to receive a changed nature, not just a change in their economic situation.

Now, some have a mistaken notion of what it means to be born again. It is:

- Not being baptized
- Not reformation
- Not becoming religious

- Not joining a church
- Not a New Year's resolution

It is a regeneration of the human spirit that was dead to spiritual things. Paul said in Ephesians 2:5, "Made us alive together with Christ." He said in Titus 3:5, "Not by works of righteousness which we have done, but according to His mercy He saved us, through the washing of regeneration and renewing of the Holy Spirit." Once we've been regenerated, we become adopted into God's family. Paul said in Ephesians 1:5, "Having predestined us to adoption as sons..." He said in Galatians 4:5, "To redeem those who were under the law, that we might receive the adoption as sons." In this scripture, to be adopted is not in the modern sense of the word, which involves a legal process. The New Testament idea is not the "making of a son," but the "placing as a son." John said in 1 John 3:2, "Beloved, now we are children of God." In short, in regeneration we receive a new life; in justification, a new standing; in sanctification, a new walk; and in adoption, a new position as a son or daughter of God. You must be born over again!

Now, the Gospel of John was written to Christians who lived in Asia Minor to sure up their faith in Jesus. John's purpose is to show how Jesus (the Logos) was empowered to break the fetters of darkness. He says in John 20:31, "That you may believe that Jesus is the Christ, the Son of God, and that believing you may have life in His name." You must be born over again! John shows us in chapter one that Jesus is the Logos, meaning the rational expression of how the Word of God became flesh and dwelled (made His tent) among us. In John 2 he shows Jesus as the miracle worker, turning water into wine. In John 3 he shows Jesus as the giver of new life because God so loved the world.

We See the Context in John 3:1

A man named Nicodemus came to Jesus by night to enquire about His identity and mission. Let me make a few passing comments about this fellow, Nicodemus:

- His name means "conqueror of the people."

- He was a Pharisee.

- He had social status as a ruler of the Jews.

- He was the teacher of Israel (John 3:10).

Now, Nicodemus came to Jesus by night. Why?

- He was fearful of what others would say.

- He was embarrassed about Jesus' appeal to the masses.

- He was curious about His teaching.

- He later becomes a believer in Jesus, according to John 19:39.

We See the Conversation in Verses 2–4

He said to Jesus, "Rabbi, we know that you are a teacher come from God; for no one can do these signs that you do unless God is with him" (v. 2). Jesus' response cut to the chase, "Unless one is born again, he cannot see the kingdom of God" (v.3).

Bible teachers typically overlook this point: Jesus' point is about the kingdom. He basically repeats His point in verse five—the kingdom. What did Jesus mean by "born again"?

When a non-Jewish person wanted to convert to Judaism, he had to be baptized first and be circumcised. This act was called being born again. Then the person was considered adopted into the Jewish faith as a proselyte. The Greek word *anothen* here means "born over again" or "born from above." The metaphor used here means that the born again experience is a work of God, whereby the Spirit of God transforms us from within. John Wesley defined it as: "The great change that God works in the soul when He brings it into life, when He raises it from the death of sin to the life of righteousness. It is a change made in the whole soul by the almighty spirit of God."[4] Nicodemus' response was in the vernacular (v. 4). This is physically impossible.

- Can one be born when he is old?
- Can one reenter his mother's womb?

The problem with Nicodemus was he couldn't comprehend spiritual realities.

We See Jesus' Instruction in Verses 5–8

Unless you're born of water and the Spirit you can't enter the kingdom of God (v. 5). This is the same point as in verse three.

What does Jesus mean by water and the Spirit? Some have interpreted this to mean Christian baptism and being Spirit-filled. Others have interpreted this to mean physical birth. In other words, before you can be born spiritually, you must first be born physically. Still, others have interpreted this to mean that one must be cleansed and filled with the Spirit's power. I believe that the "water" means the Word of God and not baptism.

> That He might sanctify and cleanse her with the washing of water by the word.
>
> —EPHESIANS 5:26

> You are already clean because of the word which I have spoken to you.
>
> —JOHN 15:3

> Sanctify them by Your truth. Your word is truth.
>
> —JOHN 17:17

47

The "Spirit" speaks of the Holy Spirit which has made us alive in Jesus Christ.

> . . . the washing of regeneration and renewing of the Holy Spirit.
>
> —TITUS 3:5

In John 3:6, Jesus provides His first illustration: "That which is born of the flesh is flesh, and that which is born of the Spirit is spirit." In other words, you can't transform the flesh in order to experience spiritual reality. There are too many Christians who are born of the flesh but think they can function in the spirit. The flesh and the spirit fight against one another, and this is the struggle which we all face, according to Galatians 5:17. The only thing you can do with the flesh is kill it. Paul said those who are led by the spirit are truly the children of God. (See Romans 8:14.)

In John 3:7, Jesus reiterates his earlier point from verse three. He tells Nicodemus, "Do not marvel that I said to you, 'You must be born [over] again.'" By *do not marvel* Jesus means don't be surprised at what I'm instructing you, Nicodemus.

In verse 8, Jesus provides His second illustration: being born over again is like the blowing of the wind. The wind blows in various directions and just because you can't see it doesn't mean it's not real. But you can hear the wind blow and you can feel the wind blow. Jesus says, "So is everyone who is born of the Spirit." After Jesus' teachings Nicodemus responds in verse nine. In his response you can sense his disbelief and frustration: "How can these things be?"

We see Jesus' response to Nicodemus in verses 10–12. Jesus is amazed that Nicodemus couldn't comprehend this spiritual truth: "Are you the teacher of Israel, and do not know these things?" Jesus continues His response to Nicodemus by adding that He is teaching a spiritual reality, which comes from God. But, Nicodemus doesn't believe Him. Therefore, Jesus says, "If I have told you earthly things and you do not believe, how will you believe if I tell you heavenly things?" (See John 3:12.)

Now, the benefits of being born over again are:

- You become a child of God.
- You are freed from guilt and shame.
- Your past sins are forgiven.
- You are filled with the Spirit.
- You are loved unconditionally by God.
- You are filled with joy.
- You obtain a crown of victory.
- You are healed.
- You will one day be glorified with Christ.
- You are more than a conqueror.

So, I believe, being born over again can turn:

- Pimps into priests
- Prostitutes into preachers
- Pushers into prophets
- Drug dealers into deacons

It can take you from the deep, dark pit of hopelessness to the mountaintop of hope. It can give you the resiliency of the energizer bunny—which keeps going and going. Some of you are experiencing fear which comes from a dark, sunless evening in your life. Even though "weeping may endure for a night, But joy comes in the morning" (Ps. 30:5). The Bible says that "many are the afflictions of the righteous, But the LORD delivers him out of them all" (Ps. 34:19). My friend, if you want to be born over again, that is, to have a fresh start; then you've got to push! For a baby to be born the woman must push through the pain! Similarly, you push through the guilt and shame; you push through the sickness; you push through the uncertainty; you push through the financial struggles; and you push through the difficult relationships. The challenge will be for you to stop procrastinating and to receive the Lord Jesus Christ. Why not do it right now!

Summary

You must be born over again! While the physical birth of a child is an amazing thing, the spiritual birth of a sinner transcends it. Since the fall of Adam and Eve, everyone after them was born into sin and corruption. The hymn says "Jesus paid it all, all to Him I owe, sin had left a crimson stain, He washed it white as snow"[5] Because of this reality you can be born over again and experience a fresh start. You see, without being born over again you'll never experience the rule of God in your life—the kingdom. The basic point of our text is that Jesus was trying to teach a religious ruler how to enter the kingdom of God. In short, Jesus was pushing Nicodemus to get over himself so that he could live a purposeful life within the kingdom.

Chapter 8

THE KINGDOM COMES IN A SEED

——❖——

Draw me, however unwilling, to make me willing; to draw me, slow-footed, to make me run.[1]

—St. Bernard

On the same day Jesus went out of the house and sat by the sea. And great multitudes were gathered together to Him, so that He got into a boat and sat; and the whole multitude stood on the shore. Then He spoke many things to them in parables, saying: "Behold, a sower went out to sow, And as he sowed, some seed fell by the wayside; and the birds came and devoured them. Some fell on stony places, where they did not have much earth; and they immediately sprang up because they had no depth of earth. But when the sun was up they were scorched, and because they had no root they withered away. And some fell among thorns, and the thorns sprang up and choked them. But others fell on good ground and yielded a crop: some a hundredfold, some sixty, some thirty. He who has ears to hear, let him hear!"

—Matthew 13:1–9

About five weeks ago I had my lawn aerated and I had fertilizer and lime placed down along with grass seed. As you know, fall is the time of year to do your yard to get it ready for the winter. The other day, I looked at the areas where I had no grass growing last year and now in those areas grass is growing. What was the difference between what I did last year and what I did this year? I aerated the yard first! Some of you are not as fruitful or productive for the kingdom because you haven't aerated the yard of your heart. That's why the seed of the Word produces no change in your life; because your heart is hard as concrete you have not learned how to get over yourself yet.

> Break up your fallow ground, And do not sow among thorns.
> —JEREMIAH 4:3

> Break up your fallow ground, For it is time to seek the LORD, Till He comes and rains righteousness on you.
> —HOSEA 10:12

As long as your heart is hard or indifferent, you'll never bear any fruit for the kingdom of God nor will you experience the blessings of God. I believe that fruitfulness for God's kingdom comes when the hard ground of your heart has been broken so that the seed of the kingdom can come into your life. The kingdom of God has already come to this world in the person of Jesus Christ. It has come like a seed. This seed will grow so the kingdom has a future culmination when Jesus returns.

I vehemently disagree with those who say that the kingdom of God hasn't come. Jesus, Himself said in Luke 17:21, "The kingdom of God is in your midst" (NAS). Some Bible teachers believe that Jesus' Second Coming is the hope of the world. No, actually it's the destruction and judgment of the world! It's the "blessed hope" of the Christian, according to Titus 2:13.

The Kingdom Comes in the Form of a Seed

Now, I believe the basic reason why we're not as fruitful for God as we ought to be is that our hearts are like fallow ground— untidy and unkempt—and weeds have grown up everywhere. Everyone knows about the fruit of the Spirit, which is found in Galatians 5:22–23, but very few know about the weeds of the flesh found in Galatians 5:16–21:

- Adultery—sexual immorality—pornography

- Fornication
- Uncleanness—impurity
- Lewdness—obscene sexual excess
- Idolatry—worship of images
- Sorcery—pharmacy, drugs, medicine
- Hatred
- Contentions—strife
- Jealousy—resentment and coveting
- Outbursts of wrath
- Selfish ambitions
- Dissension—animosity
- Heresies
- Envy
- Murders
- Drunkenness
- Revelries—carousing, rowdy, boisterous

My friend, you'll never cultivate the fruit of the Spirit as long as you allow the weeds of the flesh to grow in your life! I think the words of this hymn make my point:

> Almighty God, thy word is cast like seed into the
> ground;
> Now let the dew of heaven descend and righteous fruit
> abound;
> Let not the foe of Christ and man this holy seed
> remove,
> But give it root in every heart, to bring forth fruits of
> love.[2]

I believe one of the disturbing verses of Scripture is found in Jeremiah 8:20: "The harvest is past, The summer is ended, And we are not saved!" In other words, it's terrible when you have missed the opportunity to reap a harvest—maybe a job promotion by missing the deadline. It's passed and won't come again.

Now our text says that Jesus spoke many things to the multitude in parables. A parable is a brief story from everyday life told by way of analogy to illustrate a spiritual truth. Don't get bogged down in the particulars, but locate the main idea. To really understand this parable you have to have some idea of what it means to live in an agrarian culture. Since the industrial revolution, the United States ceased to be primarily an agrarian society. Farmers worked from sun up to sun down. They would plow the ground with an ox, and then they would take and sow seed by hand.

Jesus used ordinary examples that the people would be familiar with to articulate scriptural truth. Jesus had left the house He was staying in and sat by the sea. Why? A great multitude began to gather at the lake. Now, Jesus got into a nearby boat and began teaching the crowd by using a parable.

"Behold, a Sower Went Out to Sow"

What follows is a parable about the seed and the four types of ground it encounters.

1. Wayside ground (v. 4)
2. Stony place ground (vv. 5–6)
3. Thorny ground (v. 7)
4. Good ground (v. 8)

He closes with this statement: "He who has ears to hear, let him hear!" (v.9). In other words, if you can understand this, then understand it. Now, Jesus defines the seed as "the word of the kingdom" (v. 19). My friend, this is crucial for us to understand, because "faith comes by hearing, and hearing by the word [or seed] of God" (Rom. 10:17). And "without faith it is impossible to please [God]" (Heb. 11:6). So, let's explore what the four types of ground mean and the overall point of Jesus' message.

"Some seed fell by the wayside; and the birds came and devoured them" (v. 4).

I call this the unresponsive ground. For this type of heart spiritual things are foolishness. This person couldn't care less about Jesus, salvation, or Christianity. His heart is hard and non-responsive. Second Corinthians 4:3–4 says, "But even if our gospel is veiled, it is veiled to those who are perishing, whose minds the god of this age has blinded, who do not believe, lest the light of the gospel of the glory of Christ, who is the image of God, should shine on them."

Now, Jesus gives to us the interpretation of these four types of ground in Matthew 13:18–23. Notice verse 19: "The wicked one comes and snatches away what was sown in his heart." Because of pride the unresponsive ground refuses to be humble toward the Word of God. "Birds" mean thought life. That's why you have to chase the birds away like Abraham did in Genesis 15.

"Some fell on stony places" (v. 5)

For this type of heart there's not much ground but plenty of rocks. The seed does immediately sprout yet it has no depth of content, only fluff. So, when the sun shines:

- The plant is scorched/burned
- The roots wither away

I refer to this as the superficial ground. Notice verses 20–21: "But he who received the seed on stony places, this is he who hears the word and immediately receives it with joy; yet he has no root in himself, but endures only for a while. For when tribulation or persecution arises because of the word, immediately he stumbles." Thus, this type of ground receives the seed immediately with joy, but really doesn't have any roots and is shallow. When tribulation arises (Greek word *theipis*, which means "pressure or crushing") they aren't able to stand the heat and pressure, which cause them to stumble. If you desire to please God, you will endure suffering and hardship.

Second Timothy 3:12 says, "Yes, and all who desire to live godly in Christ Jesus will suffer persecution." *Stones* mean strongholds of sin. You've got to remove the stones from your life that hinder your relationship with God.

"And some fell among thorns, and the thorns sprang up and choked them" (v. 7).

I refer to this as the worldly ground. Notice verse 22 says: "He who hears the word, and the cares of this world and the deceitfulness of riches choke the word, and he becomes unfruitful." Paul said in 1 Timothy 6:10 "For the love of money is a root of all kinds of evil." John said in 1 John 2:16, "For all that is in the world—the lust of the flesh, the lust of the eyes, and the pride of life—is not of the Father but is of the world." So, what are your priorities?

"And others fell on the good soil and yielded a crop, some a hundredfold, some sixty, and some thirty" (v. 8).

I refer to this as the receptive ground. Notice verse 23 says, "But he who received seed on the good ground is he who hears the word and understands it, who indeed bears fruit and produces: some a hundredfold, some sixty, some thirty." The receptive ground is productive and fruitful one hundred-, sixty-, and thirty-fold.

Psalm 1:3 compares the believer to "a tree Planted by the rivers of water … And whatever he does shall prosper." Several years ago, the United States Department of Agriculture developed a soil treatment chemical that contained six percent ethyl alcohol. In the proper amounts this solution allows weeds to grow at an accelerated rate. Once the weeds grow, they can be removed before their seeds grow. Some fields have become free of weeds for up to five years. The blood of Jesus is one hundred percent divine and it can cleanse you of all the weeds in your life!

A tenant farmer had lived on a certain farm for a good many years, renewing his lease from time to time as it expired. Day by day he had been up at dawn, and worked after other men had gone to bed at night. He had fertilized and built up the soil. The fences had been kept in good repair. He had struggled valiantly to keep down the weeds. The buildings were well painted and in good condition. The orchard had been trimmed and sprayed annually, and bore the best fruit in the neighborhood. In short, it was a model farm, admired by farmers far and near.

One day the agent who looked after the land called on the farmer and notified him that he would have to vacate the place. The owner's son, who was about to be married wanted to take over the farm.

It is not difficult to imagine some of the feelings of this hardworking farmer. He made a number of offers to the owner, hoping that he might change his mind. But all his suggestions were in vain. The day was set when he must leave the place, and it seemed to him that the labor of the years had been lost to him.

In the weeks that intervened he had done some angry brooding, and had decided to get revenge. He gathered weed seeds wherever they could be found, seeds which were the pest of the farmer. Just before he was to leave the place, one dark night he moved up and down over the clean fertile fields, sowing the seeds of the noxious weeds.

The next morning, bright and early while the farmer was still doing the chores, the agent drove up. He promptly passed on the information that the owner's plans had been changed— the son had decided not to move onto the farm, and the lease could be renewed.

"What a fool I've been," the farmer exclaimed. Just what he meant the agent never knew. But the farmer knew that he would have to reap from his sowing. He knew of the hours of toil and anguish he must spend because of that one night's deed.

You and I must reap as we sow. If we sow wild oats, we cannot expect to reap the tame variety. If we sow frowns and cross words, we may expect people to shun us. Unkind criticism and backbiting won't make us friends or bring us joy. Days of toil for ourselves alone will not give us happiness. Plant kindness, courtesy, helpfulness, and you will have a joyous reaping. It is one of God's laws: "Whatever a man sows, that he will also reap" (Gal. 6:7).

Someday we will be asked to vacate our place, to go the way of all the earth. In the day of final awards, the time of reaping, you and I shall reap as we have sown. May we sow wisely.

Summary

The kingdom of God is the rule of God in the heart of His people. When you plant a seed in the ground, that seed germinates and grows. Before the seed grows the soil/ground must be receptive. Some of you have not experienced the full benefit of being a child of God because you haven't really been receptive to God's seed. When was the last time you opened the Word of God to commune with God? When was the last time you really studied God's Word? Fruitful Christians are those who are receptive to the Word of God as it is sown into their souls. You see, the kingdom of God comes in the form of a seed.

Chapter 9

TRIBULATION: DOORWAY TO THE KINGDOM

We must somehow believe that unearned suffering is redemptive.[1]

—MARTIN LUTHER KING JR.

The problem with life is that it is daily! If life were one long unending weekend it would be grand...But it ain't!

—DR. JAMES R. LOVE SR.

Then Jews from Antioch and Iconium came there; and having persuaded the multitudes, they stoned Paul and dragged him out of the city, supposing him to be dead. However, when the disciples gathered around him, he rose up and went into the city. And the next day he departed with Barnabas to Derbe. And when they had preached the gospel to that city and made many disciples, they returned to Lystra, Iconium, and Antioch, strengthening the souls of the disciples, exhorting them to continue in the faith, and saying, "We must through many tribulations enter the kingdom of God."

—ACTS 14:19–22

Trouble, problems, stress, anxiety are all terms which can be used to describe the experience of most people today. If it's not a situation at home with the children or on your job with coworkers, or tension between you and your supervisor; then, it's the car, or the toilet in the bathroom backed up again! If it's not one thing it's another! Sometimes we have what I call those days when everything seems to be going wrong.

I used to work as a school principal. I remember back in

November 1996, the day before Thanksgiving, one toilet wasn't flushing in the boys' bathroom, one of my teachers had to leave for an emergency, an irate parent was in my office, and in one of the classrooms a plumbing pipe burst and flooded one of the mobile units. That was a dreadful day! We've all had days like that.

I believe that the most difficult thing about life is that it is daily. If life were just the weekends and holidays, it would be wonderful. But life is Monday through Friday facing situation after situation, problem after problem. It is what Shakespeare called "the slings and arrows of outrageous fortune." Unfortunately, some have developed an escapist mentality by trying to flee from their problems. They are like the proverbial ostrich, believing that if they keep their head in the sand, all their problems will just go away. Cult groups, like the Christian Scientists, teach that evil is an illusion, sickness is a matter of mind over matter, and if you confess positive things, all your troubles will go away. Yeah, right!

T. S. Eliot was correct when he wrote, "humankind cannot bear very much reality."[2] My friend, don't be deceived. If you're going to live as a believer in Jesus Christ, you will experience stresses, troubles, and all manner of problems. You have an adversary who wants to make things difficult for you.

Now, we all experience times of tribulation. However, for the believer these times are the doorway to the kingdom of God. Tribulations will either make you better or bitter! It will either draw you closer to Jesus Christ or repel you away.

1 Peter 4:12–13 says, "Beloved, do not think it strange concerning the fiery trial which is to try you, as though some strange thing happened to you; but rejoice to the extent that you partake of Christ's sufferings, that when His glory is revealed, you may also be glad with exceeding joy." Somebody reading these words right now has been in the storm too long. Hang in there; trouble won't last forever. "Weeping may endure for a night, But joy [will come] in the morning" (Ps. 30:5). Psalm

46:5 says "God is in the midst of her, she shall not be moved; God shall help her, just at the break of dawn."

My friend, you'll never know the power of God to overcome your adversities and tribulations until you've been through the wilderness. Some of you are at the "p.m." of your life, characterized by the prevailing darkness all around you, like a harbinger announcing: "It's all over for you, no more dreams, no more victory, and no more seeing the light of a new day." But God has vouchsafed to me in this book, this message: you will no longer see the p.m. but the a.m. of a new day approaching! Hear the promise of God concerning the a.m. of a new day in Isaiah 43:1–3:

> Fear not, for I have redeemed you; I have called you by your name; You are Mine. When you pass through the waters, I will be with you; And through the rivers, they shall not overflow you. When you walk through the fire, you shall not be burned, Nor shall the flame scorch you. For I am the LORD your God, The Holy One of Israel, your Savior…

Again, we all have been in trouble at one time or another in our lives. Do you remember the time when you were in grade school and the teacher sent you to the principal's office? How about the time you misplaced your wedding ring? What about the time you went to the mall and forgot where you parked? Remember the time you went out to dinner and when it was time to pay the bill you discovered that your credit card was maxed out and you had no cash? All the above are situations that have caused us trouble and no small amount of embarrassment.

Acts 15:19–22 is a story about the troubles of the great missionary, the apostle Paul. Acts 13–14 records Paul's first missionary journey to Galatia. He and Barnabas had been sent out by the Spirit, according to Acts 13:2. There was a great anointing upon Paul and Barnabas to preach the gospel, but there was also great opposition and persecution.

Wherever Paul and Barnabas went they had either a revival, revolution, or revolt. The Jews would stir up trouble wherever Paul and Barnabas showed up.

In Acts 14:1–7, great signs and wonders were being done in Iconium, but the Jews sought to kill the apostles. They fled. In verses 8–17, in the town of Lystra a crippled man was healed, and the citizens thought that Paul and Barnabas were gods. Again the Jews stirred the people to opposition against them. Verse 19 says, "Then Jews from Antioch and Iconium came there; and having persuaded the multitudes, they stoned Paul and dragged him out of the city, supposing him to be dead."

People will "stone" you with their words of criticism, innuendoes, and character assassination. People will talk about you and leave you for dead. Whenever you strive to do God's will, most of your opposition won't come from the unbeliever, but from religious folks! Trust me on this.

Verse 20 says, "However, when the disciples gathered around him, he rose up and went into the city." When you've been stoned by religious folks, that's the time you need the disciples to gather around you. The support from others is so crucial after people or life situations have thrown stones at you. The text says that Paul went to another city named Derbe with Barnabas (v. 20). I believe that Paul had a mission from God, and he was so full of the Spirit that he simply refused to die!

Verse 21 says, "And when they had preached the gospel to that city and made many disciples, they returned to Lystra, Iconium, and Antioch." Paul preached the gospel to these other cities with great success. The content of his message came out of his experience of being stoned.

Verse 22 says, "Strengthening the souls of the disciples, exhorting them to continue in the faith, and saying, 'We must through many tribulations enter the kingdom of God.'" What does Paul mean? The Greek word for *tribulation* is *thlipsis*. It means "crushing, squashing, squeezing like a wine press/meat grinder." This word is used in John 16:33.

Now, we must never forget that although we are triumphant and victorious in this life, it doesn't come without hurt, pain, and suffering. Sometimes you're going to cry a while. Sometimes you're going to be disappointed. Sometimes you're going to experience the emptiness of a broken heart. Sometimes you're going to be misunderstood and ostracized. Any view that teaches that life as a Christian is like a tiptoe through the tulips is a lie! Job said in Job 14:1, "Man who is born of woman Is of few days and full of trouble." But, I thank God that a little later in this same chapter, in verse 14, Job said, "All the days of my hard service I will wait, Till my change comes." He also said in Job 13:15, "Though He slay me, yet will I trust Him."

David said in Psalm 34:19, "Many are the afflictions of the righteous, But the LORD delivers him out of them all." My friend, the reality is that at some point in your Christian walk, you're going to be in the midst of a storm. It may not be because of anything you did wrong. It may just be that God wants you to experience His rule and dominion in your life. Through many tribulations we enter into the kingdom of God. In short, tribulation is the doorway into the kingdom of God! I assure you that once you've been through the wilderness—through the storm—God becomes more real to you than ever before. Remember the contemporary parable of the man who saw his footprints in the sand? Jesus carried him through his most difficult trial.

Paul said it so well in 2 Corinthians 4:8–9: "We are hard-pressed on every side, yet not crushed; we are perplexed, but not in despair; persecuted, but not forsaken; struck down, but not destroyed." Tribulation is the doorway to the kingdom of God. You see, the school of suffering and hard knocks graduates wise scholars. Moreover, you can't have a testimony until you've had a "test-a-many." When you get to heaven, God won't look at your degrees, medals, or awards; He'll look for scars. My friend, it's going to cost you to be used by God!

Paul said it right in Galatians 6:17, "Let no one trouble me, for I bear in my body the marks of the Lord Jesus." Therefore, at the end of the day I can sing the words of that great old hymn of the church: "Just another day that the Lord has kept me, He has kept me from all evil with my mind stayed on Jesus...Just another day."[3] Sometimes, in the midst of the tribulation, I can hear this song ringing in my spirit:[4]

> I've had some good days, I've had some hills to climb,
> I've had some lonely days and some sleepless nights.
> But when I look around and I think things over,
> all of the good days outweigh my bad days,
> I won't complain.
> You see, God has been good to me, more than anyone
> could ever be.
> He dries my tears away, turns my midnight into day;
> so I say thank you Lord I won't complain.

In other words, I can summarize this song: tribulation = the doorway to the kingdom of God.

Finally, can the gospel of the kingdom really dissolve deep-seated prejudices that have been hardened by centuries of hatred and strife? The experience of Yishael Allon of West Valley City, Utah, gives the answer. Yishael is Jewish. About 17 years ago, he met his cousin's wife Sandy, who was dying of leukemia. Peace filled her heart and a love radiated from her life that gave her a "special glow."

"She was the first real Christian I had ever met," writes Yishael. "She was different. I would question her, and all she'd talk was Jesus." In 1980, Yishael heard the gospel on the radio and received a Bible. As he read Isaiah 53, the Holy Spirit convinced him that the prophet was speaking about Jesus—the same Jesus that Sandy knew. Yishael recalls, "I believed in the Lord Jesus and became a 'completed Jew.'" Now here's the answer to the question of prejudice. Yishael says, "A year and a half later, the Lord gave me His love for my enemies—the PLO who murdered thirty-seven of my friends."[5]

Chapter 10

THE KINGDOM IS IN THE HOLY SPIRIT

═➤◆⇐═

The purpose of life is not to win. The purpose of life is to grow and to share. When you come to look back on all that you have done in life, you will get more satisfaction from the pleasure you have brought to other people's lives than you will from the time that you outdid and defeated them.[1]

—RABBI HAROLD KUSHNER

For the kingdom of God is not meat and drink; but righteousness, and peace, and joy in the Holy Ghost.

—ROMANS 14:17, KJV

Someone once said that a text without a context is simply a pretext. Our text occurs in Romans where Paul is teaching about the righteousness of God, which is "imputed" to believers through the work of Christ on the cross. In Romans 14, Paul addresses two major themes: Christian liberty (v. 1–12) and Christian love (v. 14–23).

Regarding Christian liberty, Paul's point is: don't become judgmental of the freedom in Christ as some Christians have. Some worship God silently, some loudly, some worship on one day while others on another day. His point is that no one lives to him or herself, we live unto the Lord; so stop judging one another because we all must appear before the judgment seat of Christ ("judgment" is *bema* in Greek). A great Christian credo that I live by is: in essentials, unity; in the non-essentials, liberty; and in all things, love. So I am taken back at how some Christians can be so critical and pedantic in lambasting another brother or sister without compunction or regret.

Therefore, those who truly desire to get over themselves and to live a purposeful kingdom lifestyle must reject the human proclivity to be judgmental and critical of another brother or sister in Christ.

Now, regarding Christian love; Paul's point is if you know meat offends your brother or sister, then in their presence abstain from eating meat. He says that if you refuse to abstain from what clearly is your right and prerogative, then you are deficient in your love for Christ and for that brother or sister. This is precisely the point of verse 15, which he reiterates in 1 Corinthians 8:13.

Then he makes this statement in verse 16: "Do not let your good be spoken of as evil." What does this verse mean? Basically, if you're strong in the faith and you've discovered that there's freedom in Jesus Christ (not to sin); yet another brother or sister who may not be as strong will be offended by your freedom in Christ. Those who are strong must choose to willingly refrain from certain freedoms so that they aren't spoken of as evil, in the sense that it weakens the faith of a brother or sister. To say this another way: get over yourself!

Thus, Paul says in Romans 15:1, "Now we who are strong ought to bear the weaknesses of those without strength and not just please ourselves" (NAS). So then, "the kingdom of God is not eating and drinking, but righteousness and peace and joy in the Holy Spirit" (Rom 14:17). What does Paul mean by this verse? If I were to perform surgery upon this verse in order to get at its essential meaning, I would exegetically disembowel it by surgically removing the phrase "...is not eating and drinking, but righteousness and peace and joy..." Righteousness is what Christ gives to us at salvation, the benefits of which are peace and joy. Now, what remains of this verse would be this: "the kingdom of God...in the Holy Spirit."

Who Is in Charge?

When Jesus Christ walked on the earth, He was the personification, the embodiment, or in Latin the *vox dei* (voice of God) of the kingdom of God. Thus, wherever He went, there went the kingdom. When He performed miracles, raised the dead, and fed the multitudes, He was demonstrating the transcended power of God's rule over the destructive works of Satan. Jesus said in John 10:10, "The thief does not come except to steal, and to kill, and to destroy. I have come that [you] may have life [*zoe*], and that [you] may have it more abundantly." Also, John said in 1 John 3:8, "For this purpose the Son of God was manifested, that He might destroy the works of the devil."

Fundamentally then, the kingdom is all about who is in authority: God or Satan? Before Jesus died, He gathered His disciples and told them He was leaving them, but He assured them that He would send them another paraclete (or helper) called the Holy Spirit. He said that *they* would do greater works than He did (see John 14:12) because the third person of the Godhead—God the Holy Spirit—would give them the authority to extend His kingdom agenda. It is as Dr. Myles Monroe said, "Man was created with gifts and divine nature to execute God's will in the earth. The ultimate goal of God the creator was to colonize earth with heaven and establish it as a visible territory of an invisible world."[2]

Now, on that momentous day of Pentecost, God the Holy Spirit descended like fire and the disciples were filled with the Spirit, spoke in tongues, and witnessed three thousand people added to their ranks.

Who Is the Holy Spirit?

I think for us to gain the Biblical and the theological comprehension of the phrase "in the Holy Spirit," we need to examine the person and the work of the Holy Spirit. The Holy Spirit is a person with whom you can have a personal and dynamic relationship. Too many Christians see the Holy Spirit as some sort of force; similar to what was popularized by the Star Wars trilogy's motto "May the force be with you." The Holy Spirit isn't a "force" or an "it" or a "feeling." He is the dynamic presence of almighty God. The Holy Spirit is very God. The church has generally neglected the Holy Spirit in its creeds and dogmas. Except for a brief statement in the Apostle's Creed, the Holy Spirit was neglected for the first nineteen hundred years of church history. It was not until the beginning of this century that the Holy Spirit began to receive serious theological attention. With the 1906 Azusa Revival, which birthed the Pentecostal movement, the Holy Spirit then became center of the church's attention.[3]

Now, in the Old Testament, the Holy Spirit was active in creation, and He would empower men and women to achieve great things for God. For example, the Holy Spirit inspired David to write beautiful songs and poetry. Samson's great strength was given by the Holy Spirit. Bezaleel, in Exodus 31:2–5, was anointed to build the tabernacle. But, if you read the Old Testament closely, you will discover that the Holy Spirit did not abide with these individuals; He was only manifested temporarily.

Once again, when we talk about the Holy Spirit, we are talking about the third person of the Godhead. We are talking about a part of the Trinity. This is one doctrine that is essential for us to believe if we're going to have a biblically sound view of God. Some have accused Christians of worshiping three Gods. They say we are not monotheist but polytheist. To set the record straight: I believe in one God who is revealed in three persons; Father, Son, and Holy Spirit. One being who is revealed in three distinct *persona* (Latin). In Greek dramas actors would put on different masks to give the character personality. God is one (*homoousios*) being, yet manifested in three *persona*.

The Father isn't the Son and the Son isn't the Father; neither is the Father the Holy Spirit nor the Holy Spirit the Son. The Father works in creation, the Son works in redemption, and the Holy Spirit works in sanctification. Another way to communicate this is: the Father thinks it, the Son speaks it, and the Holy Spirit performs it.

The Bible certainly teaches the doctrine of the Trinity. For example:

- "Let us make man..." (Gen 1:26).

- "I heard the voice of the Lord, saying: 'Whom shall I send, And who will go for Us?'" (Isa. 6:8).

- "Baptizing them in the name of the Father and of the Son and of the Holy Spirit" (Matt. 28:19).

- "The grace of the Lord Jesus Christ, and the love of God, and the communion of the Holy Spirit be with you all" (2 Cor. 13:14).

You see, the Holy Spirit is not less than God; He is eternal God! The Holy Spirit is "holy." The Greek word is *hagios* meaning "pure, separated, complete." (There are unholy spirits called demons.) Once again, the Holy Spirit is not a force, feeling, power, or an "it," but a person who can be grieved, hurt, and rejected.

Now, what is the work of the Holy Spirit? John 16:7–14 gives us an excellent description. The chief work of the Holy Spirit is to glorify Jesus Christ:

- By teaching about Christ
- By drawing people to Christ
- By reproducing Christ's character in us
- By directing Christians into service
- By empowering Christians to witness
- By convincing the unrighteous about their sin

In Him

You see, unless you comprehend the role of the Holy Spirit in your life you will never become a victorious Christian. The enemy of your soul wants to criticize and berate you so that you focus upon your problems like a panic-struck deer that is caught gazing into a car's headlights before being hit. But the Holy Spirit wants you to look up and see your help coming from the Lord. My friend, you need the power of the Holy Spirit to live this Christian life! You need the guidance that comes from the Holy Spirit because you don't know how to run your life, but He does!

Paul said in 2 Corinthians 4:7 that God has placed "this treasure in earthen vessels." This speaks of the treasure of the Holy Spirit within us. I say this with tongue in cheek; we can all become like a crackpot because of various situations in life. But rest assured that "He who has begun a good work in you will complete it" (Phil. 1:6). Through the power of the Holy Spirit that resides within us, we have been given authority to do kingdom business. Every morning when you get up you ought to invite the Holy Spirit to lead and guide you throughout the day. Get over yourself, and don't be wise in your own understanding. Instead, let the Spirit come into every situation and circumstance in your life.

Did you know that the New Testament says some 164 times that we are "in Christ" or "in Him" and that Christ is in us? How?—by the Holy Spirit. Take to heart the following scriptures:

- Ephesians 1:4—chosen in Him
- 1 Corinthians 7:22—called in Him
- Ephesians 2:5—made alive in Him
- Romans 5:1—justified in Him
- Ephesians 2:10—created for good works in Him
- 1 Corinthians 1:2—sanctified in Him
- Romans 6:5—assured of the resurrection in Him

- Romans 3:24—redeemed in Him
- Romans 6:23—eternal life in Him
- 1 Corinthians 1:30—righteous in Him
- Galatians 2:4—freedom in Him

You see, it is the work of the Holy Spirit to glorify Him—Jesus Christ!

The fable, "The Lion and the Three Bulls," written by the Greek fable writer Aesop, gives insight into how important it is for teammates to be communicative. Three bulls lived together for a long time in a pasture. Though they ate and lived side by side, they never spoke with one another. One day a lion came along and saw the bulls. The lion was very hungry, but he knew that he could never attack three bulls at once because together they would overpower him and kill him. So the lion approached the bulls one at a time. Since one bull never knew what the others were doing, they didn't realize that the lion was working to separate them. The lion, which was crafty, succeeded in dividing them, and with them successfully isolated, he attacked them individually. Thus he overcame all three of them and satisfied his hunger.[4]

The moral of this story is that the enemy of our souls wants to divide us from each other in order to destroy. If the bulls could have gotten over themselves and worked together; they could have defeated their adversary the lion. So, similarly, if we cooperate with the Holy Spirit we will be able to defeat our enemy, Satan.

An Overdose of the Holy Spirit

Please excuse my colloquialism: I believe, right now what some of you need is an overdose of the Holy Spirit! Some of you need to stop getting high on wine, money, sex, and status, and get high on the Holy Spirit! There is a popular Gatorade commercial that has as its slogan "Is it in you?" The implication is that drinking Gatorade will give you a competitive edge over your opponent. I've changed it around somewhat to say: "Is He in you?" Now, I am talking about the Holy Spirit. He will give you the victory over your opponent the devil. My friend, in order to defeat your spiritual adversary you had better have more than a shout and more than your good looks; you had better have Him in you! Is He in you? My prayer for you is that the Spirit of God will fall afresh on you.

> Live out Thy life within me, O Jesus, King of kings!
> Be Thou Thyself the answer to all my questionings;
> Live out Thy life within me, in all things have Thy way!
> I, the transparent medium, Thy glory to display.
>
> The temple has been yielded, and purified of sin,
> Let Thy Shekinah glory now shine forth from within,
> And all the earth keep silence, the body henceforth be
> Thy silent, gentle servant, moved only as by Thee.[5]

Chapter 11

SEEK FIRST THE KINGDOM

—⊰◈⊱—

If there is no immortality of the soul, there can be no
virtue and therefore everything is permissible.[1]
—FYODOR DOSTOYEVSKY

But seek first the kingdom of God and His righteousness, and all these things shall be added to you.
—MATTHEW 6:33

It is said that success can be defined as the progressive
realization of a predetermined goal. To be successful one has
to prioritize the really important things against those things
that are not so important. Buying a new dress or suit may not
be as important as paying your rent or mortgage. Spending
extra time at work may not be as important as spending time
with your children. Spending Sunday morning at home isn't
as important as spending time with your heavenly Father at
church. I believe that good things often are the enemy of God-
things. I believe God will bless the God-things because only
God-things please God! Hebrews 11:6 says, "Without faith it
is impossible to please [God]."

It is said that we ought to "keep the main thing, the main
thing." This is a matter of your priorities. Are they the things of
God or the things of this world? That's why Paul said in Colossians 3:1–2: "If then you were raised with Christ, seek those
things which are above, where Christ is, sitting at the right
hand of God. Set your mind on things above, not on things on
the earth."

Years ago it was said (pejoratively speaking) that so-and-
so is so heavenly-minded that they are no earthly good. Now,

today, we are so earthly-minded that we are no heavenly good! Your priorities ultimately determine your lifestyle. Look at certain lifestyles—the rich and famous, the upper class or even the middle class—and how they set goals to achieve their priorities. I have said for years, when you compare the priorities of an unbeliever with those of a believer there is little or no difference! In other words, many believers are just as materialistic; they need to get the car, the house, the clothes, and the money, just as their unbelieving counterpart.

Unfortunately, there are too many believers who do not have any spiritual priorities or goals. When it comes to natural things, such as personal goals, job advancement, and budgets, we set goals and establish priorities. But when it comes to spiritual things, such as prayer, Bible study, fasting, and giving, we do not make these priorities. Point of fact: many Christians do not have any spiritual priorities. Thus, we give God our leftovers—leftover time, leftover effort, leftover talents, and leftover money. In Malachi 1:7–8 the people offered leftover offerings to the Lord.

> You offer defiled food on My altar, But say, "In what way have we defiled You?" By saying, "The table of the LORD is contemptible." And when you offer the blind as a sacrifice, Is it not evil? And when you offer the lame and sick, Is it not evil? Offer it then to your governor! Would he be pleased with you? Would he accept you favorably?" Says the LORD of hosts.

We tend to think about spiritual things as less important, so we do not take them as seriously as other things in our lives. I believe that if you don't give greater priority to spiritual things you will end up chasing lesser earthly things and end up frustrated. It reminds me of the story of a school of three hundred whales that suddenly died. The whales were pursuing sardines and found themselves marooned in a bay. One reporter said, "The small fish lured the sea giants to their death... They came to their demise by chasing small ends." Some of you are like those whales that chased after small sardines, which can lead to your destruction.

Now, because we have gotten our priorities out of kilter, we suffer the consequences, which are worry and anxiety. In other words, misplaced priorities will lead to misplaced goals, which lead to misplaced values, which lead to misplaced choices, which lead to misplaced trust, which lead to worry and anxiety.

Although the Master said in Matthew 6:25, "Do not worry," if we are honest, this is a difficult thing not to do. Because we have fallen so far from the ideal standards of God, our weakened humanity forces us to worry and be anxious. The reason we worry is because certain things are out of our control and power. We worry about whether we locked the front door; we worry about the weather; we worry about crime in our neighborhood; we worry about what we look like; we worry about getting older; we worry about our money; we worry about our children; we worry about our husbands; we worry about our wives; we worry about our health; we worry about what people say or think about us; we worry about being worried! My advice to you is this: get over yourself and discover what it means to live purposefully in the kingdom of Jesus instead of living me-centered in this world.

And, my friends, it is this lack of control which really bothers us. We must be in control. So whenever we lose control we worry. The fact is you can worry yourself to death, but not to life. Dr. Charles Mayo, of the famous Mayo Clinic, once wrote, "Worry affects the circulation, the heart, the glands, the whole nervous system. I have never known a man who died from overwork, but many who died from doubt."[2] In addition, one doctor reported that worry could lead to stomach ulcers and to coronary thrombosis.

It's Time to Seek First the Kingdom!

Let's widen our text now to include Matthew 6:25–34. In this wider context you will discover that the Master is teaching about how misplaced priorities lead to worry and anxiety. It reminds me of the story of a group of people who were going to climb Mont Blanc in the Alps of France. The guide said to the climbers that they could only take the bare necessities in their backpacks. But there was one American who said no and took a bunch of unnecessary stuff. He took off first. As the group got to the hardest part of the climb they noticed all sorts of items along the way. So when they reached the top of the mountain the American was there minus all his extra stuff. The point is if you are going to strive for the kingdom, you've got to get over yourself. You've got to put aside all the unnecessary weight. And you've got to make the kingdom your priority. Hebrews 12:1 tells us to "lay aside every weight, and the sin which so easily ensnares us."

Worry is unfruitful because of who Jesus is (v. 25).

Jesus gives us a command to not worry. He repeats it five times in verses 25, 27, 28, 31, and 34. The Greek word *merimnao* means "to divide into parts, distraction, and preoccupation with things causing anxiety and stress." God gives to us life; therefore, He can be trusted with lesser things. It is inconsistent to trust God for your eternal future but not trust Him to put food on your table. Jesus' point is that life is much more than the acquisition of material things. My friend, worry is unfruitful because of who Jesus is. Regarding this point, let's look at what the Scriptures promise:

> My God will supply all your needs according to His riches in glory in Christ Jesus.
>
> —PHILIPPIANS 4:19, NAS

For you know the grace of our Lord Jesus Christ, that though He was rich, yet for your sakes He became poor, so that you through His poverty might become rich.

—2 CORINTHIANS 8:9

Cast your burden on the LORD, And He shall sustain you; He shall never permit the righteous to be moved.

—PSALM 55:22

Worry is unnecessary because of who our Father is (vv. 26–30).

Jesus uses this illustration by asking us to consider the birds of the air. They aren't stressed about food or what they need to survive because your heavenly Father takes care of the birds. "Are you not of more value than they?" (v. 26). Jesus says you are more valuable to God than birds. He feeds them, He will feed you. He goes on to ask, "Which of you by worrying can add one cubit to his stature?" (v. 27). Jesus' point is simple: worry is a useless emotion that doesn't change anything.

He gives His second illustration about our worry over clothing. Jesus says, "Consider the lilies of the field" (v. 28). I believe Jesus loved flowers. The lilies that Jesus is referring to were probably scarlet poppies. They bloomed for one day or so and were quite beautiful. After they finished blooming people would gather them in baskets to fuel a fireplace or stove. Although these lilies have a short lifespan they are very beautiful. Their beauty surpasses the ornate glory of King Solomon.

In referring to King Solomon, perhaps Jesus had in mind 1 Kings 10:4–7:

And when the queen of Sheba had seen all the wisdom of Solomon, the house that he had built, the food on his table, the seating of his servants, the service of his waiters and their apparel, his cupbearers, and his entryway by which he went up to the house of the LORD, there was no more spirit in her. Then she said to the king: "It was a true report which I heard in my own land about your words and your wisdom. However I did not believe the words until I came and saw with my own eyes; and indeed the half was not told me. Your wisdom and prosperity exceed the fame of which I heard."

Therefore, if God has so masterfully beautified these short-lived flowers, how much more will He beautify you, "o you of little faith" (v. 30)? In other words, get over yourself and let the Father beautify you in His kingdom. My friend, worry is unnecessary because of who our Father is. I've always taken great comfort in what the apostle Peter said in 1 Peter 5:7, "Casting all you care upon Him, for He cares for you."

Worry is unreasonable because of our faith (vv. 31–33).

Jesus says don't worry about eating, drinking, and your clothing needs. Your heavenly Father knows you need these things. To worry about these things indicates your lack of faith. Jesus' point is that these basic necessities of life are what heathens focus on. Now, observe Jesus' statement in verse 33: "But seek first the kingdom of God and His righteousness, and all these things shall be added to you." Jesus' point is that one must be willing to reorganize one's priorities from eating, drinking, and clothing, to the kingdom.

Paul said in Romans 14:17, "For the kingdom of God is not eating and drinking, but righteousness and peace and joy in the Holy Spirit." The kingdom must be your number one priority in your vocation, whether as a secretary, teacher, lawyer, or doctor. Your priorities must not be the acquisition of more money or stuff, but on demonstrating how a kingdom person acts, looks, and behaves. Along this line, I disagree with these priority charts which have God, home, work etc., in a descending order. The Bible makes no such declaration. There are only two priorities in the believer's life: the kingdom and righteousness. What does all this mean? Seeking the kingdom means to lose oneself in obedience to the Lord to the extent of Paul's words in Acts 20:24: "Nor do I count my life dear to myself, so that I may finish my race with joy, and the ministry which I received from the Lord Jesus, to testify to the gospel of the grace of God."

What is your passion? What drives you? My friend, you know your priorities are correct when the rule and the purposes of God are foremost on your mind. Can you truthfully say that you are sold out to Jesus Christ? You see, the secret to getting over yourself is to live under the rule of Jesus Christ.

Now, regarding righteousness, Paul said in Philippians 3:9, "And be found in Him, not having my own righteousness, which is from the law, but that which is through faith in Christ, the righteousness which is from God by faith." Righteousness is a gift from God through the sacrifice of Jesus Christ whereby God declares a sinner in right standing in his or her relationship to Him. All these things will be added unto you when you seek the kingdom and His righteousness. The very things you were worried about will seek you out! Deuteronomy 28:1–14 talks about the blessings and the provisions of obedience to God's kingdom.

Worry is unwise because God has a future plan for us (v. 34).

Because you are actively seeking the kingdom and His righteousness, don't worry about tomorrow. Sometimes we worry about the future: "How's this going to work out?" or "How's that going to work out?" You can become so preoccupied about tomorrow that you forget about today. Focus on what you have today, and tomorrow will take care of itself. Psalm 90:12 teaches "us to number our days, That we may gain a heart of wisdom."

Jeremiah 29:11–14 says:

> For I know the thoughts that I think toward you, says the Lord, thoughts of peace and not of evil, to give you a future and a hope. Then you will call upon Me and go and pray to Me, and I will listen to you. And you will seek Me and find Me, when you search for Me with all

your heart. I will be found by you, says the LORD, and I will bring you back from your captivity; I will gather you from all the nations and from all the places where I have driven you, says the Lord, and I will bring you to the place from which I cause you to be carried away captive.

You must keep in mind that God has a wonderful plan for your life. I reiterate the point: worry is unwise because God has a future plan and destiny for your life!

Like a river glorious, is God's perfect peace,
Over all victorious, in its bright increase;
Perfect, yet it floweth, fuller every day,
Perfect, yet it groweth, deeper all the way.

Hidden in the hollow of His blessed hand,
Never foe can follow, never traitor stand;
Not a surge of worry, not a shade of care,
Not a blast of hurry touch the spirit there.

Stayed upon Jehovah, hearts are fully blest
Finding, as He promised, perfect peace and rest.[3]

Finally, there are eleven things that this text teaches us about worrying:

1. Worry is useless as an emotion.
2. Worry indicates an unawareness of God's providence.
3. Worry indicates an unawareness of God sovereignty.
4. Worry really doesn't help the situation.
5. Worry leads to fear.
6. Worry and fear mean negative faith.
7. Worry leads to physical sicknesses.
8. Worry indicates lack of trust.
9. Worry denies the fatherhood of God.
10. Worry denies the goodness of God.
11. Worry indicates misplaced priorities.

I believe it is our misplaced priorities that give worry its power. But Jesus' point is to redirect your priorities and you won't have cause to worry. It reminds me of the story in Luke 10:38–42 that tells of Mary and Martha and the choice they each made. Martha was more concerned about the logistics of a meal than the eternal Logos. Mary chose the Logos over logistics.

Finally, how do I combat worry?

> Be anxious for nothing, but in everything by prayer and supplication, with thanksgiving, let your requests be made known to God; and the peace of God, which surpasses all understanding, will guard your hearts and minds through Christ Jesus.
>
> —PHILIPPIANS 4:6–7

> Do not fret because of evildoers, nor be envious of the workers of iniquity. For they shall soon be cut down like the grass, And wither as the green herb. Trust in the LORD, and do good; Dwell in the land, and feed on His faithfulness. Delight yourself also in the LORD, And He shall give you the desires of your heart.
>
> —PSALM 37:1–4

Don't allow worry or anxiety to rob you of the blessings God has for you. You will obtain the blessing only if you seek first the kingdom. In other words, get over yourself and learn to live worry-free as you find the kingdom-purpose for your life.

Chapter 12

WHAT DO YOU DO WHEN YOU GET ANGRY?

—◆—

Anger is a universal experience. Everyone will either get angry or is already angry.

—DR. JAMES LOVE

Therefore, putting away lying, "Let each one of you speak truth with his neighbor," for we are members of one another. "Be angry, and do not sin": do not let the sun go down on your wrath, nor give place to the devil.

—EPHESIANS 4:25–27

For approximately five years I served as the school administrator for Covenant Christian Day School in Greensboro, North Carolina. I had many wonderful experiences interacting with my staff of teachers, the students, and the parents. One of the more challenging experiences was when I met James (not his real name) for the first time. He was a second-grader who was full of energy; your typical boy! But James had a problem: he would get out of control with rage! Further, when he got angry he would get physical. Many times I was called in to deal with James because something was said or done by a classmate, which triggered his rage. Typically I would remove him from the situation, walk with him around the building and let him talk out what was bothering him. It was clear to everyone that James had a mean temper.

In 1968, two black psychiatrists, William H. Grier and Price M. Cobb, wrote a provocative book called *Black Rage*.[1] This book looks at the affects of methodical dehumanization of black people in America in the 1960s, and offers a cogent justification for their rage.

What is anger? According to *Merriam-Webster's New Collegiate Dictionary* (Sixth Edition), it has been defined as: "A strong passion or emotion of displeasure, and usually antagonism, excited by a sense of injury or insult."[2] Anger is always stimulated by an event. Typically this anger is then expressed in behavior by word or action. Thus, anger is a cluster of emotions:

- From irritation to indignation
- From bitterness to resentment
- From revenge to rage

When you are angry your adrenal gland produces hormones that stimulate your heart rate, blood pressure, and lung function.

What is the origin of anger? Why is anger so universal? I believe our capacity for anger is rooted in the nature of God. We are created in the image of God and so we reflect some of His characteristics.

1. God is holy. That means He is separate and apart from sin. (See Leviticus 11:44–45 and 1 Peter 1:16.)

2. God is love. In His essential being God is loving. (See 1 John 4:8.) Be careful not to misunderstand as some do that *love is God.*

God's anger is derived from His essential nature, which reacts to evil, injustice, and unrighteousness. So, I believe our God-given ability to get angry arises whenever we encounter what we perceive to be wrong. Dr. Gary Chapman states in his book, *The Other Side of Love: Handling Anger In a Godly Way*: "What is God's purpose for human anger? I believe the answer is clear: Human anger is designed of God to motivate us to take constructive action in the face of wrongdoing or when facing injustice."[3] For example, in Jeremiah 3:12–14 we read how God's anger motivates Him to send the prophet Jeremiah to call the people to repentance. One thing that must be kept in mind here is that there are three types of anger: 1.) Definitive anger is our emotional response toward any kind of genuine wrongdoing, mistreatment, or injustice upon us; 2.) Distorted anger is our emotional response toward any kind of perceived wrongdoing, mistreatment, or injustice upon us; 3.) Displaced anger is anger at others who are not a part of the situation. Allow me to illustrate each one...

- Definitive Anger: The promotion you should have received is given to someone less qualified. You were mistreated in a restaurant because of your race. A close friend lies about you or betrays a deep trust.

- Distorted Anger: The computer crashes and you lost two hours worth of work! The lawn mower breaks down. Cain felt anger toward his brother Abel.

- Displaced Anger: You're angry about something, yet you take it out on those around you, such as your wife or friends, who did not cause the anger. They simply become the object of your anger.

You deal with distorted anger by asking: 1) Was a wrong committed? 2) Do I have all the facts? and 3) By taking a moment to breath and release the tension and stress.

Ephesians 4:26–27 says, "When angry, do not sin; do not ever let your wrath (your exasperation, your fury or indignation) last until the sun goes down. Leave no [such] room or foothold for the devil [give no opportunity to him]" (AMP).

The New English Bible reads: "If you are angry, do not let anger lead you into sin; do not let sunset find you still nursing it; leave no loop-hole for the devil" (NEB). Notice that God gives you the permission to get angry. Let me make several observations about this: anger is a God-given emotion, anger isn't necessarily sinful, and anger must have safeguards such as: 1.) Do not let the sun go down on your anger, and 2.) Do not give the devil an opportunity.

So now, when is anger justified? When God's people knowingly disobey God's Word and will. In Matthew 21:13 Jesus drives the moneychangers out of the temple. In Mark 3:4–5 Jesus heals the man with the paralyzed hand and becomes angry with the Pharisees because of their legalism. Their concern for the law and their lack of compassion for the paralyzed man caused Jesus to react with anger.

Anger is justified when there is a reversal of the moral order of God: Isaiah 5:20–25. Call good bad and right wrong; for example gay marriages are accepted and virginity is laughed at.

Anger is justified when children are unfairly dealt with by parents. (See Ephesians 6:1–4.) Paul is warning parents, specifically fathers, not to strike or provoke their children to anger.

Anger is justified when injustice and unrighteousness prevail. (See Micah 6:6–8.) The Lord requires us to do justly, love mercy, and walk humbly with God.

Conversely, anger is unjustified when it comes from the wrong motives. For example, the older brother of the prodigal son was angry. (See Luke 15:28.) Anger is unjustified when you're angry because things aren't going your way. Jonah was angry because God spared the city of Nineveh. (See Jonah 4:2–4.) Anger is unjustified when we react to a situation too quickly without investigating all the facts. Ecclesiastes 7:8 says, "The end of a thing is better than its beginning." James 1:19 puts it this way: "But everyone must be quick to hear, slow to speak and slow to anger" (NAS).

So how do we handle our anger?

False ways

- Denial = I am ok. I am not angry.

- Camouflage = I am not angry but disappointed.

- Passive/Aggressive = Outwardly no big deal but inwardly great turmoil.

True ways

- Consciously acknowledge your anger.

- Learn to ignore petty disagreements. "A man's discretion makes him slow to anger" (Prov. 19:11, NAS).

- Refrain from close association with anger—prime people. Proverbs 22:24 says, "Make no friendship with an angry man." 1 Corinthians 15:33 says it this way: "Evil company corrupts good habits."

- Keep very close check on your tongue. James 1:19 says, "Everyone must be quick to hear, slow to speak and slow to anger" (NAS). "A soft answer turns away wrath" (Prov. 15:1).

- Cultivate honesty in communication... don't let anger build up. "Faithful are the wounds of a friend" (Prov. 27:6).

Finally, I believe anger will destroy you and all those around you. It reminds me of a "Dear Abby" column that appeared in the *St. Paul Pioneer Press Dispatch*. It reads:

> Dear Abby: A young man from a wealthy family was about to graduate from high school. It was the custom in that affluent neighborhood for the parents to give the graduate an automobile. Bill and his father had spent months looking at cars, and the week before graduation they found the perfect car. Bill was certain that the car would be his on graduation night. Imagine his disappointment when on the eve of his graduation Bill's father handed him a gift-wrapped Bible! Bill was so angry that he threw the Bible down and stormed out of the house. He and his father never saw each other again. It was the news of his father's death that brought Bill home again. As he sat one night going through his father's possessions that he was to inherit, he came across the Bible his father had given him. He brushed away the dust and opened it to find a cashier's check, dated the day of his gradu-

ation—in the exact amount of the car they had chosen together.[4]

God's Word, and even the trials and tests we experience, are often the wrappings of more valuable gifts the Father has in store for us. Taken at face value, they often represent what we do not want. But if we dare open them and approach them with the right attitude, we find that God has given us our dreams. He ends up giving us ourselves, enlarged and developed beyond anything we could ever muster in our own strength.

Chapter 13

FORGIVING: IT'S IN YOUR BEST INTEREST

Coming together is a beginning. Keeping together is progress. Working together is success.[1]

—HENRY FORD

For if you forgive men their trespasses, your heavenly Father will also forgive you. But if you do not forgive men their trespasses, neither will your Father forgive your trespasses.

—MATTHEW 6:14–15

In 1981 there was an assassination attempt upon Pope John Paul II. He later met with the young man who attempted to kill him. The Pope forgave him and even kissed his feet. What an act of forgiveness!

My wife has taught me a unique way to ask for forgiveness: "Please forgive me for my foolishness!" Then I'd tell her specifically what I had done. She wouldn't permit me to say, "I'm sorry." Being sorry is what got me into trouble in the first place!

Forgiving isn't easy, and by nature we find it very hard to do. Now the concept of forgiving is one of the great gifts that God has given to human beings. For without forgiving—and its cousin repentance—there can't be a second chance.

Without forgiving we would be unable to start over again. Think about that for a moment:

1. No more second chances with God...when you sin you would immediately face judgment.

2. No more second chances in relationships.

3. No more second chances to correct mistakes.
4. No more second chances to start life over again.

As I said before, forgiving is God's great gift to us and it ought to be our great gift to one another. Genuine forgiveness runs deep. It is not a thin surface patch on a relationship, but an inner change of heart toward the offender. Too often we think we have extended forgiveness when we have only covered over our resentment.

Rabbi David A. Nelson likes to tell the story of two brothers who went to their rabbi to settle a long-standing feud. The rabbi got the two to reconcile their differences and shake hands. As they were about to leave, he asked each one to make a wish for the other in honor of the Jewish New Year. The first brother turned to the other and said, "I wish you what you wish me." At that, the second brother threw up his hands and said, "See, Rabbi, he's starting up again!"

When you understand the power of forgiving, your relationships will never be the same. I agree with Jerry Cook who wrote in *Love, Acceptance and Forgiveness*:

> Love, Acceptance and Forgiveness—These three are absolutely essential to any ministry that will constantly bring people to maturity and wholeness. If the church is to be the force for God in the world that it should be, it must learn to love people, accept them and forgive them.[2]

Unfortunately, in too many church situations forgiveness is the last thing one would receive.

The word *forgive* is used 142 times in the Bible. This word is really the by-product of the word *agape*, which describes the God-kind of love—unconditional. The problem with the word *forgiving* is that it suffers from being jaded by overuse and misunderstanding. Because it is so misunderstood the power behind the word has lost its potency. Forgiving in the minds of most people, is impotent of real meaning; it is about as powerful as the common greeting "hello" or "how are you doing today?"

So, then what is forgiving? The Greek word *aphiemi* means "to let go, pardon, release, cancellation of an offense." So, forgiving means the taking of no account of the offense committed and the full acceptance of the person back into fellowship. A good illustration of this is the words of David in Psalms 103:2–3, 12: "Bless the Lord, O my soul, And forget not all His benefits: Who forgives all [my] iniquities ... As far as the east is from the west, So far has He removed our transgressions from us."

God not only lets go, pardons, releases, and cancels our sin debt, but He reinstates us back into full fellowship. I know this statement is taking some poetic license here, but you could say God develops divine amnesia!

So, because we have often misunderstood what forgiving is, a word about what it is not seems in order.

1. Forgiving isn't forgetting
2. Forgiving isn't excusing
3. Forgiving isn't going along to get along
4. Forgiving isn't accepting or liking the person
5. Forgiving isn't tolerating people

To forgive a person who has wronged you is really to extend to them grace that they don't deserve. But keep in mind that I don't deserve the grace of God either! Lewis Smedes, in his book *Forgive and Forget*, says there are four stages in forgiveness:[3]

1. We hurt...the initial offense
2. We hate...the person who causes the offense
3. We heal...as time passes we move on
4. We reconcile...at some point we allow the offender back into our lives

About fifteen years ago another pastor and I worked with Kim (not her real name). She was thirty years old. She had been molested as a fourteen-year-old by her father and by her uncle. She was very angry and bitter. Though years had passed, she struggled to maintain any male relationships. She hated her father. Worst of all, she felt responsible! Eventually with a few years of counseling she was slowly able to forgive her father. Last I heard she is working for an agency that addresses the issues facing battered and sexually abused women. I could see her coming through the process of hurt, hate, healing, and eventually reconciliation when she started to forgive her father.

I believe forgiving is very important in the development of any relationship. In fact, you won't have much of a relationship if you don't learn how to forgive. When you search the pages of sacred Scripture you will discover a plethora of examples of people who had to learn how to forgive in order that God might use them:

1. Jacob had to seek forgiveness from his brother Esau because of how he had deceived him, if he was going to fulfill his God-given purpose (Genesis 33:4.)

2. Joseph, who had been mistreated by his brothers, had to forgive them if he was going to fulfill his God-given purpose (Genesis 50:20).

3. Stephen, the first Christian martyr, was being stoned to death and asked God not to charge his murderers with the sin of stoning him (Acts 7:60).

Again, you see the key to understanding forgiving is that the offender doesn't deserve it, but you must grant it because it's in your best interest! When you forgive someone you must forgive him or her from your heart and not from your head.

Unforgiveness is like a cancer that eats away at you from the inside, and it is progressive:

- Hurt leads to anger...
- Anger leads to hate...
- Hate leads to bitterness...
- Bitterness leads to revenge...
- Revenge leads to...
- Self destruction.

Some people have been carrying offenses and unforgiveness for years. The problem here is that probably the person who has offended or hurt you hasn't thought about you or the hurt they caused! But it's still fresh in your mind. This hinders purposeful kingdom-living. Perhaps this is what Jesus had in mind in Matthew 5:23–24:

> Therefore if you bring your gift to the altar, and there remember that your brother [or sister] has something against you, leave your gift there before the altar, and go your way. First be reconciled to your brother [or sister], and then come and offer your gift.

My friend, to the extent we have been forgiven by God we ought to forgive one another. For me to fail to forgive myself or anyone else who has offended me is to imply that I have a higher standard of forgiveness than God, because whatever it is that has so hurt me that I can't forgive it, God already has. 1 John 1:9 says, "If we confess our sins, He is faithful and just to forgive us of our sins and to cleanse us from all unrighteousness."

Also, in Colossians 3:13 the apostle Paul said, "Bearing with one another, and forgiving one another, if anyone has a complaint against another; even as Christ forgave you, so you also must do."

Notwithstanding, I think the clearest and most cogent teaching about forgiveness ever taught was by Jesus Christ in Matthew 18:21–35. Peter questions Jesus about forgiving: "How often shall my brother sin against me, and I forgive him? Up to seven times?" (v. 21). Jesus responds to Peter's question by saying, no! You have it all wrong. It's not about quantity of forgiving but the quality of forgiving which is extensive. It's not about counting, but about character, Peter! Therefore, not seven times but seven times seventy (490 times a day) (v. 22)! In addition, Jesus gives an illustration about forgiveness (vv. 23–35). A king forgave a large debt by one of his servants. Later that servant sees another servant who owes him a small debt. The servant with the small debt begs for more time but is tossed into prison. Now when the other servants witnessed this they informed the master. When the master saw the servant he was angry and ordered that he be turned over to the torturer. Unforgiveness always leads you to the torturer—people are stressed, anxious, with ulcers due to worry, irritable because of unforgiveness.

Finally, Jesus concludes with an ominous warning in verse 35: "So My heavenly Father also will do to you if each of you, from his heart, does not forgive his brother his trespasses."

Allow me to give you a personal illustration of this truth. In 1994 when I was the school administrator at Covenant Christian Day School in Greensboro, North Carolina, I learned a valuable lesson about myself and how difficult forgiveness is. A parent had a delinquent account of two thousand dollars! I tried everything I could to appeal to the man's Christian ethics to pay the bill. He made several excuses. So I called him one last time to pay up. He got indignant, and then I got indignant! The rest of the day my spirit was uneasy. The Lord told me to call the man back and to apologize to him! I refused. But by the end of the day I did. Consequently, in a short period of time he ended his delinquent account by paying in full. Once I got over myself, my pride in other words, I learned a lesson about how to live a purposeful kingdom-life in a me-centered world.

Forgiving isn't easy, and by nature we find it very hard to do. But the ultimate example of forgiving is the death of Jesus Christ on the cross of Calvary. Let me enumerate some of the injustices He endured:

1. Falsely accused by religious leaders
2. Scourged by the Roman soldiers
3. Spat upon
4. Mocked
5. Betrayed
6. Rejected
7. Forsaken by friends and by God
8. Beaten
9. Nailed to a cross
10. Stabbed in the side
11. Left to die between two criminals

And yet, in Luke 23:34, he said, "Father, forgive them, for they do not know what they do."

Right here, the words of the old hymn seem appropriate: "Must Jesus bear the cross alone and all the world go free? No. There's a cross for everyone and there's a cross for me."[4] You and I must embrace the command to forgive. You can't divorce forgiveness from love. And fundamentally the Christian community is a community of love.

So, why should I forgive? Why is it in my best interest?

1. It's a biblical injunction from God...

2. It will release you from the spirit of bitterness and anger...

3. It offers the opportunity for reconciliation...

4. It is an act of love...

5. It offers the opportunity for a second chance.

Forgiving isn't easy, and by nature we find it very hard to do. But forgiving is what we must do because it's in our best interest. I believe you can really monitor whether or not you've gotten over yourself by how prone you are to readily forgive.

Epilogue

NINE PRACTICAL PRINCIPLES ON HOW TO GET OVER YOURSELF

━━━➤◆◅━━━

First: Resist the Evil Eye of Jealousy and Envy

I think the spirit that best characterizes our present culture is jealousy or envy. Just look at the rise of reality TV programs: "The Bachelor," "Survivor," "The Apprentice," etc., all focus upon the spirit of jealousy, envy, and competition.

Not long ago I read a story about a young boy who stabbed another boy over a pair of Air Jordan tennis shoes! I don't believe that we can ever get over ourselves and embrace a purposeful kingdom lifestyle without addressing the problem of jealousy and envy. What is jealousy and what is envy?

Actually, envy and jealousy are a form of covetousness. They are a violation of the tenth commandment: "You shall not covet..." (Exod. 20:17).

Jealousy is a strong displeasure over the advantages or prosperity of others. Envy is a feeling of discontent and *resentment* aroused by *thinking* of another's possession or qualities, with a strong desire *to have them* for oneself.

Sometimes when you look at the lifestyles of others and you compare them with your own, you can become jealous of the success of others. You see, jealousy and envy are emotions. When they are not held in check they can lead to anger and bitterness. Allow me to be blunt: you don't have to be jealous of anyone because what God has for you is for you.

95

The Bible has a lot to say about envy and jealousy. For example listen to:

- Proverbs 27:4: "...Who is able to stand before jealousy?"

- Romans 13:13: "Let us walk properly ... not in lewdness and lust, not in strife and envy."

- Galatians 5:21: The works of the flesh are "envy, murders ..."

- 1 Timothy 6:4: "He is proud ... from which come envy, strife, reviling, evil suspicions..."

- Titus 3:3: "...Living in malice and envy, hateful and hating one another."

My friend, it was envy and jealousy that motivated the religious rulers to turn over Jesus to Pilate in Matthew 27:18 and Mark 15:10. It was envy and jealousy that motivated King Saul to throw a spear at David in 1 Samuel 18:8–11. I believe many church schisms are directly related to envy and jealousy by somebody within the church. In Matthew 20:15 Jesus asks the question: "Or is your eye evil because I am good?" Also, in Mark 7:21–22, He says, "For from within, out of the heart of men, proceed evil thoughts...an evil eye."

Matthew 20:1–16 is commonly called the "Parable of the Workers in the Vineyard." Ultimately, the point of this parable is about the sovereignty of God granting rewards to His servants. Those workers who started at the beginning of the day supposed that they would receive more than those workers who started at the end of the day. Yet, in this scripture we observe a fundamental attribute of God—His love—which gives grace to those who don't deserve it. So, I view this passage as a sterling illustration of the great compassion and overflowing generosity of God.

Finally, how do I overcome the spirit of jealousy and envy? Read Paul's prescription for jealousy in Philippians 2:1–10.

1. Realize who you are and what God has given to you…

2. Rejoice with those who rejoice and weep with those who weep…

3. Express to others how much you appreciate the talents and gifts within them…

4. Stop just looking at the bad in people; try to see some good…

5. Pray for the welfare of others.

Second: Understand Biblical Authority and Submission

Now when Jesus had entered Capernaum, a centurion came to Him, pleading with Him, saying, "Lord, my servant is lying at home paralyzed, dreadfully tormented." And Jesus said to him, "I will come and heal him." The centurion answered and said, "Lord, I am not worthy that You should come under my roof. But only speak a word, and my servant will be healed. For I also am a man under authority, having soldiers under me. And I say to this one, 'Go,' and he goes; and to another, 'Come,' and he comes; and to my servant, 'Do this,' and he does it." When Jesus heard it, He marveled, and said to those who followed, "Assuredly, I say to you, I have not found such great faith, not even in Israel! And I say to you that many will come from east and west, and sit down with Abraham, Isaac, and Jacob in the kingdom of heaven. But the sons of the kingdom will be cast out into outer darkness. There will be weeping and gnashing of teeth." Then Jesus said to the centurion, "Go your way; and as you have believed, so let it be done for you." And his servant was healed that same hour.

—Matthew 8:5–13

The mark of a kingdom person is submission to authority. Jesus is the King of the kingdom and His followers are His subjects. One cannot possess authority until it is given and until they are under authority. Jesus has given to certain men and women delegated authority. We don't have problems with Jesus' authority, but we do with His delegated authority. Now, in the incarnation God was in Christ. The face of God is seen in the incarnate Jesus who is the living Word. We must understand that God uses people to do His work. If you ever comprehend the incarnation at work, then you will say, like Paul says in 2 Corinthians 5:18, that God was in Christ reconciling the world to Himself.

Why Do People Resist Authority?

1. Spirit of rebellion
2. Lack of discipline
3. Don't understand God's order
4. Abuse of authority

How Do We Define Authority?

Ted Engstrom's book, *The Making of a Christian Leader*, says, "We have to understand authority. A common but well-reasoned definition is: authority is whatever you possess at the moment that causes someone else to do what you want him to do at that moment."[1] I believe that authority is the legal right to act in a manner which accomplishes a task. For example, the police have full authority and backing from the city to act in order to enforce the laws of the city.

Therefore, there are four types of authority, according to some leadership experts. First, there is authority of *competence*. This is a person who is in a position of leadership because of their skills at getting things done. This person may be an excellent manager or organizer. Second, there is the authority of *position*. This is a person who is in leadership by virtue of an appointment. This person has authority simply because they have the title. Third, there is authority of *personality*. This person is a leader by virtue of who they are as a person; perhaps they have a charismatic personality that attracts others to them. Finally, there is the authority of *character*. In other words, this person is a leader by virtue of their character or those qualities that people most admire about them.

Watchman Nee, in his book *Spiritual Authority*, said, "As God's servants, the first thing we should meet is authority. God's authority represents God Himself."[2] Along this same line, Hebrews 13:7, 17 states:

> Remember those who rule over you, who have spoken the word of God to you, whose faith follow, considering the outcome of their conduct....Obey those who rule over you, and be submissive, for they watch out for your souls, as those who must give account. Let them do so with joy and not with grief, for that would be unprofitable for you.

Thus, the kingdom person is open and willing to yield to legitimate authority within the church. The word *submit* in the Greek is *hupotasso*, which means "to be yielded, to stand under"; thus, ultimately submission is an attitude or disposition. For example, 3 John helps us to see the different responses to authority and submission:

- Gaius: godly lifestyle, walks in truth, gracious towards saints and strangers, submissive (vv. 1–8).

- Diotrephes: selfish ambition, rejects authority, authoritarian practices, ungracious, unsubmissive (vv. 9–11).

- Demetrius: good testimony, submissive, walks in truth (v. 12).

Finally, in Acts 4:19 Peter and John teach that the believer must choose to obey God's authority rather than man's. I believe that within the kingdom authority is more relational than positional. The better your relationship, the more authority you will possess. Fundamentally, I believe authority is given or delegated. To take authority is to be in a state of rebellion. I believe the real basis of one's authority in the kingdom is one's character or walk, and not one's position or talk.

Third: Servanthood

> Then James and John, the sons of Zebedee, came to Him, saying, "Teacher, we want You to do for us whatever we ask." And He said to them, "What do you want Me to do for you?" They said to Him, "Grant us that we may sit, one on Your right hand and the other on Your left, in Your glory." But Jesus said to them, "You do not know what you ask. Are you able to drink the cup that I drink, and be baptized with the baptism that I am baptized with?" They said to Him, We are able." So Jesus said to them, "You will indeed drink the cup that I drink, and with the baptism I am baptized with you will be baptized; but to sit on My right hand and on My left is not Mine to give, but it is for those for whom it is prepared." And when the ten heard it, they began to be greatly displeased with James and John. But Jesus called them to Himself and said to them, "You know that those who are considered rulers over the Gentiles lord it over them, and their great ones exercise authority over them. Yet it shall not be so among you; but whoever desires to become great among you shall be your servant. And whoever of you desires to be first shall be slave of all. For even the Son of Man did not come to be served, but to serve, and to give His life a ransom for many."
>
> —MARK 10:35–45

Then Jesus called a little child to Him, set him in the midst of them, and said, "Assuredly, I say to you, unless you are converted and become as little children, you will by no means enter the kingdom of heaven. Therefore whoever humbles himself as this little child is the greatest in the kingdom of heaven."

—MATTHEW 18:2–4

I have a definite conviction about the need to return to biblical servanthood. Here are a few of my thoughts:

1. In the kingdom the pathway to greatness is by servanthood. The world recognizes greatness by those who serve; for example, Mother Theresa or Martin Luther King, Jr. Servanthood has recently fallen on hard times. People aren't as faithful to serve as they once were. Perhaps the reason we don't see servanthood the way it used to be is due to lifestyle changes. Priorities are different, and we don't stress it as much.

2. The Greek word for *servant* is *doulos*, which means "bondage or slavery." Paul calls himself a "bondservant" in Romans 1:1, Philippians 1:1, and Titus 1:1. It meant "to be a slave by choice" (the idea here of a love slave). In the kingdom everyone is a servant. The office of deacon is an office created in Acts 6 to be a serving component of the apostle. The Greek word *diakonia* means "to attend, to wait upon another."

3. Examples of servanthood: Joshua was Moses' servant (Joshua 1:1); Elisha served Elijah; Timothy served Paul. Look at how Jesus served His disciples in John 13:1–5, 15, and 17. Fundamentally, I believe the only way we can recapture the spirit of servanthood is if we recognize the need for humility. We need to become like children: trusting, dependent, and humble. In simple terms, we need to get over ourselves if we are to become good servants of Jesus Christ.

Four: Righteousness

> For I say to you, that unless your righteousness exceeds
> the righteousness of the scribes and Pharisees, you will
> by no means enter the kingdom of heaven.
>   —MATTHEW 5:20

The righteousness required for entrance into the future realm of God's kingdom is a present righteousness; a righteousness which exceeds that of the scribes and Pharisees, says Jesus. It is a righteousness that only God can impart once He takes up His reign in your life. Scribes were writers, professional students of the law. Pharisees were those who accepted the teaching of the scribes, attempted to live out their teaching, and had a strong desire to be righteous. Scribes and Pharisees tried to legislate every aspect of life. Moreover, they were sticklers for obeying the Ten Commandments, which they had over the centuries expanded to over six hundred laws!

The Greek word for "righteousness" is *dikaiosune*, which means "just, the quality of being right." God declares the believer who has been acquitted and imparts righteousness to him. This is forensic (judicial) and relational. Now, what did Jesus mean by this statement: "Unless your righteousness exceeds"? What is this greater righteousness required to enter the kingdom? Allow me to postulate the following four points:

The rule of anger

The sixth commandment says don't murder. Jesus makes anger tantamount to murder. (See Matthew 5:21–22.) Now, a truly righteous person seeks to avoid anger. The righteousness of the kingdom is an internal one; whereas, the righteousness of the Scribes and Pharisees is external. It is a matter of the heart. In the kingdom, what you are is more important than what you do. Is anger sin? No. Murder is anger full grown. The righteousness of the kingdom requires right relationships, so reconciliation and forgiveness are crucial (vv. 23–24).

The rule of purity

The seventh commandment forbids adultery. Jesus makes lust tantamount to adultery. (See Matthew 5:27–30.) Looking at a woman with desire equals lust, and lust means sin. The act has already been done in the heart. Righteousness, in the form of sexual purity, begins in the heart. Jesus says using hyperbole (literary technique of exaggeration) do whatever it takes to keep your heart pure.

The rule of honesty

The ninth commandment forbids bearing false witness. Jesus says if you have to swear by oath to keep your word, this indicates you're dishonest. Don't confuse this with the oath one takes in a court of law (not the same context). The Jews had developed a system of oath-taking to demonstrate honesty and truthfulness. Yet, one could break an oath without any guilt because some of the objects of the oath were considered more sacred and thus binding. For example, as a kid, everybody knows when you swear on your mother's grave, that is a serious oath. Jesus is saying that if you have to swear by an oath, then you really can't be trusted. Let your "yes," mean yes and your "no" mean no. (See Matthew 5:33–37 and Deuteronomy 6:10–20.)

The rule of love

How do you react or respond when you have been wronged? Do you turn the other cheek (see Matthew 5:38–42) and love your enemies (see Matthew 5:43–48)? Jesus is saying that kingdom righteousness requires us to be free of the spirit of retaliation and revenge. Kingdom righteousness is motivated out of love that extends forgiveness. Jesus' point is that all deeds must always be motivated out of love.

In closing, Matthew 5:20 challenges us to realize that kingdom righteousness requires more than outward deeds, but an inward disposition. If a tree is rotten on the inside, although it looks healthy on the outside, it is still destined to fall. Kingdom righteousness is an inward righteousness of the heart. It is an inner disposition that yields to the King. Matthew 5:48 says, "Therefore you shall be perfect, just as your Father in heaven is perfect."

Five: Justice

> He has shown you, O man, what is good; And what does the LORD require of you But to do justly, To love mercy, And to walk humbly with your God?
> —MICAH 6:8

Justice is at the heart of the kingdom. The Old Testament has much to say about the poor, the oppressed, and about how God will judge those who mistreat them. (See Psalm 10:16–18; 72:1–4; 82:1–4; 113:5–7; 146:7–10.) In ancient times most of the people were poor and they often sold themselves into slavery just to survive.

Luke 4:18–19 says, "The Spirit of the LORD is upon Me, Because He has anointed Me To preach the gospel to the poor; He has sent Me to heal the brokenhearted, To proclaim liberty to the captives And recovery of sight to the blind, To set at liberty those who are oppressed; To proclaim the acceptable year of the LORD." Jesus states His mission in ministry.

The kingdom does have social justice implications. Justice is a major biblical theme. The Old Testament prophets like Amos spoke about injustice and oppression. Amos 5:24 says, "Let justice run down like water, And righteousness like a mighty stream." Psalm 89:14 says, "Righteousness and justice are the foundation of your throne." I believe the church should lead the parade on social health issues like senior citizen retirement, welfare to work, and educational reform.

In his book, *A Kingdom Manifesto*, Howard Snyder mentioned the following ways in which the church can manifest the law of justice:[3]

1. Christians are called to meet the needs of the poor within the church. Romans 15:26; 2 Corinthians 8; Acts 4:34–35

2. Kingdom Christians will work for justice in government policies that affect the poor. This means advocacy ministry.

3. Kingdom Christians must proclaim Jesus Christ as Savior and liberator of the poor and oppressed.

Proverbs 21:13 says, "Whoever shuts his ears to the cry of the poor Will also cry himself and not be heard."

Six: Paradox

But many who are first will be last, and the last first . . . So the last will be first, and the first last. For many are called, but few chosen.

—MATTHEW 19:30; 20:16

A paradox is a true statement that appears self-contradictory. Jesus used paradox all the time in His teaching. For example, He said unless a grain of wheat dies, it won't live to produce. Or, He told the rich man to sell all his wealth and become poor to gain true riches. Or, unless you take up your cross and die, you won't have true life. We struggle with paradoxes because we like things to be either/or, this or that, black or white. But sometimes life has a lot of gray areas.

To live in the kingdom means to live with the reality of paradox. The world teaches one way of thinking, but the kingdom teaches us an entirely different way of thinking. For example: the world says, "Hate your enemies," the kingdom says, "Love." The world says, "Hit back." The kingdom says, "Do good to those who mistreat you." The world says, "Hold onto your life at any cost." The kingdom says, "Lose your life and you will find it." The world says, "A young and beautiful body is essential." The kingdom says, "Even a grain of wheat must die if it is to have life." The world says, "Push yourself to the top." The kingdom says, "Serve if you want to lead." The world says, "You are number one." The kingdom says, "Many who are first will be last and the last first." The world says, "Acquire gold and silver." The kingdom says, "Store up treasure in heaven if you would be rich." The world says, "Exploit the masses." The kingdom says, "Do good to the poor."

This principle of the kingdom certainly challenges our culture-ingrained way of thinking. The kingdom of God is an inverted kingdom, or as one scholar referred to it—the upside down kingdom. This is certainly evidenced by some of the above-referenced comments. I fundamentally believe that the secrets to getting over one's self is to live under the kingdom rule of God. The implication of this is most radical because you have to live in such a way that embraces paradox.

Seven: Peace

> You will keep him in perfect peace, Whose mind is stayed on You, Because he trusts in You.
> —ISAIAH 26:3

I believe the heart of kingdom and a key to getting over yourself is this idea of peace. Our world is constantly in a state of turmoil and conflict. People struggle to relate to one another; and tension fills our jobs, churches, homes, and neighborhoods. Anxiety and stress are major problems in the lives of most. What many people are looking for is peace. The kingdom is ruled by One who is called "the prince of peace" (Isa. 9:6).

Paul said in Romans 14:17, "The kingdom of God is not eating or drinking, but righteousness and peace and joy in the Holy Spirit." The Hebrew word *peace* is *shalom*, which means "the absence of conflict, harmony, to be whole." Jeremiah 33:6 says, "Behold, I will bring it health and healing; I will heal them and reveal to them the abundance of peace and truth." The Greek word *eirene* means basically the same as *shalom*.

Howard Snyder, in his book *A Kingdom Manifesto*, says, "In God's kingdom plan, peace is both in the final goal of the kingdom and the present experience of the community of Jesus' disciples."[3] What does the Scripture teach about peace in the kingdom? Let me suggest to you four principles:

Perfect peace

In Isaiah 26:3 the "perfect peace" referred to is contingent upon a steadfast focus and an unwavering trust upon Yahweh. When you reflect upon the faithfulness of God, the writer alludes He will keep you focused upon Him in the difficult situations and trials within your life.

Jesus' peace

In John 14:27, Jesus said that He has in His authority to grant His disciples peace. He says, "My peace I give to you." This peace would sustain them through the shock of Jesus leaving them. Moreover, every challenge they would face they would be able to handle knowing Christ has granted them His supernatural peace.

Peace with God

In Romans 5:1, Paul states the blessed benefits of justification. He says we have "peace with God." The basic idea here is that humankind has been defeated and God has won the war. To say this another way: as an unbeliever, you were at war with God. Now, through the gospel of Jesus Christ, the unbeliever has been subdued by the grace, mercy, forgiveness, and love of God! Thus, "peace with God" is a result of the battle between the unbeliever, who now is a believer, acknowledging to God, "You have won, I surrender."

God of peace

In addition, Paul states on two occasions (Romans 16:20 and Philippians 4:7) that the believer can experience the "God of peace" in any situation or trial that confronts them. In the midst of trouble or persecution there's the confidence in knowing that God is there within you and He will grant to the believer peace. Peace is one of the attributes of God in the same way love is.

The church must first be at peace with itself. Also, the church must present a gospel of peace to the world, not a message of violence, distrust, discord, and alienation. Therefore, the sooner we get over ourselves, the sooner we can become God's unique agents of peace in a world gone crazy!

Eight: Priority

> But seek first the kingdom of God and His righteousness, and all these things shall be added to you.
> —MATTHEW 6:33

> Brethren, I do not count myself to have apprehended; but one thing I do, forgetting those things which are behind and reaching forward to those things which are ahead, I press toward the goal for the prize of the upward call of God in Christ Jesus.
> —PHILIPPIANS 3:13–14

If you are going to be a kingdom person, then you are going to need to get your priorities straight! Too many Christians are worldly in their priorities. Sometimes in talking to a nonbeliever and to a Christian about their lifestyles and priorities, you would be hard-pressed to see any difference. Most are worried about their jobs, finances, etc. Now, just like you, I have seen charts written by some Christian attempting to establish a hierarchy of priorities:

1. God
2. Family
3. Church
4. Job
5. Self

I fundamentally disagree with such charts because I believe God could have given us a priority list if it was necessary. There is only one priority, and our text identifies it very clearly—the kingdom of God! The context of our text in Matthew 6:33 is discussed in greater detail in chapter ten. But, briefly, Jesus is teaching about the folly of worry for those who are in the kingdom. It would be beneficial to read the following verses, which reiterate this point: Matthew 6:25, 27, 28, 31, 34. I contend that when your priorities are wrong, they lead to worry. I believe the only priority of the believer is to seek first the kingdom of God and His righteousness!

Therefore, to worry is a sin. Kingdom people have their priorities together. Worry is the result of mixed-up priorities. Paul's point in Philippians 3:13–14 is that the mark of Christian maturity is not to focus on past failures or mistakes. I believe Paul's mentality went something like this: "one thing I do"; in other words, I make this one thing my priority—the call of God. Now, what are your priorities?

Nine: Prayer

And when you pray, you shall not be like the hypocrites. For they love to pray standing in the synagogues and on the corners of the streets, that they may be seen by men. Assuredly, I say to you, they have their reward. But you, when you pray, go into your room, and when you have shut your door, pray to your Father who is in the secret place; and your Father who sees in secret will reward you openly. And when you pray, do not use vain repetitions as the heathen do. For they think that they will be heard for their many words. Therefore do not be like them. For your Father knows the things you have need of before you ask Him. In this manner, therefore, pray: Our Father in heaven, Hallowed be Your name. Your kingdom come. Your will be done On earth as it is in heaven. Give us this day our daily bread. And forgive us our debts, As we forgive our debtors. And do not lead us into temptation, But deliver us from the evil one. For Yours is the kingdom and the power and the glory forever. Amen. For if you forgive men their trespasses, your heavenly Father will also forgive you. But if you do not forgive men their trespasses, neither will your Father forgive your trespasses.

—MATTHEW 6:5–15

Now it came to pass, as He was praying in a certain place, when He ceased, that one of His disciples said to Him, "Lord, teach us to pray, as John also taught his disciples." So He said to them, "When you pray, say: Our Father in heaven, Hallowed be Your name. Your kingdom come. Your will be done on earth as it is in heaven. Give us day by day our daily bread. And forgive us our sins, For we also forgive everyone who is indebted to us. And do not lead us into temptation, But deliver us from the evil one."

—LUKE 11:1–4

One day, as Jesus was praying, His disciples asked Him how they should pray. Jesus didn't offer them a model prayer but an outline for an effective prayer life. He contrasts the praying of people and groups around Him. Remember, in the culture in which Jesus lived, prayers were said several times a day. So the disciples knew about prayer. But Christ's prayers were somehow different than those around them. Jesus seemed to posses a unique relationship with God the Father that was based upon intimacy and fellowship. As a result, Jesus seemed to get His prayers answered! In other words, God responded to Jesus' prayers.

Our Lord said in Matthew 6:5, "And when you pray, you shall not be like the hypocrites." In all likelihood Jesus is referring to Matthew 6:2; the hypocrites gave their charitable deeds to be seen by people. In a similar manner they prayed to be seen by people; thus, they were hypocrites. To be a hypocrite meant "to pretend, to play act, to read a script." The Greek word is *hupokrites*, which refers to an actor who wore a mask in a drama. The *hupokrites* always concealed his or her true motives. Jesus cites two problems with hypocrites who try to pray: 1) They love to stand in the synagogues and on every street corner. 2) They love to be seen by people. Jesus says about these people that they already have their answer. What is their answer? Nothing!

Our Lord said in Matthew 6:7, "Do not use vain repetition as the heathen do." The heathen were those who were either non-religious or the semi-religious folks. They practiced their religion only on certain religious days. Jesus said the problem with this group is they use vain repetition. This is empty babble; repeating a long prayer over and over. In other words, verbosity is meaningless! This type of prayer is designed to produce frenzy and hysteria.

The approach to prayer must be to find a quiet place to pray in secret. Observe the same language in verses 4, 6, and 18 about the Father who sees in secret and who listens. The "room" or "closet" is not to be taken literally, but as conveying the idea of getting away in secret. Thus, in Matthew 6:5–15, Jesus instructs His disciples to pray according to this outline:

I. Three heart desires toward God

    A. "Our Father in heaven" means God's name (v. 9).

    B. "Your kingdom come" means God's kingdom (v. 10).

    C. "Your will be done" means God's will (v. 10).

II. Three requests for ourselves

    A. "Give us this day our daily bread" (v. 11).

    B. "Forgive us our debts, As we forgive our debtors" (v. 12).

    C. "Do not lead us into temptation" (v. 13).

III. Three praises for the answered prayer

    A. "Yours is the kingdom" (v. 13).

    B. "And the power" (v. 13).

    C. "And the glory forever. Amen" (so let it be; it is so) (v. 13).

In verses 14 and 15, observe Jesus' comments on the importance of forgiveness as it relates to receiving answers to prayer. God's love and forgiveness are always available to you. But they have one condition: you must forgive! When you cease to forgive God likewise will cease to forgive you. Hence, to the extent you have been forgiven, similarly you must forgive. Herein is a fundamental reason why so many Christians don't receive an answer to their prayers; they hold on to unforgiveness and grudges! I believe that those who refuse to let go of offense, grudges, and hurts from the past, clearly demonstrate that they haven't gotten over themselves.

FINAL WORDS

⟫◆⟪

"Thy Kingdom come, Thy will be done"

Your kingdom come. Your will be done On earth as it is in heaven.

—MATTHEW 6:10

Then the seventh angel sounded: And there were loud voices in heaven, saying, "The kingdoms of this world have become the kingdoms of our Lord and of His Christ, and He shall reign forever and ever!"

—REVELATION 11:15

We have been discussing the kingdom of God and the various laws of the kingdom. We've also discovered what it means to get over yourself so that you can live a purposeful kingdom lifestyle. I reiterate what I said earlier, that the secret to getting over yourself is to live under the kingdom rule of God. The context for Matthew 6:10 is that the disciples had asked Jesus to teach them how to pray. Jesus begins by teaching them the difference between how the hypocrites pray versus the way His followers should pray.

"Thy kingdom come..."

The kingdom is the rule and reign of God in the heart of God's people. My friend, this petition is for God's kingdom to come. There is a certain sense in which God is asking us to invite His will into each situation. Where is this kingdom to come? Allow me to suggest a few areas:

- My personal lifestyle
- My church

- My family
- My job
- My neighborhood

When is the kingdom to come? Right here, right now. How is the kingdom to come?

- Commitment to God's agenda
- Communion with God's purpose
- Consecration for God's service

My friends, you must make a deliberate choice. It reminds me of the time I was writing a paper for a religion class. When I ran the spell check, the word "Jesus" came up. The spell check said that that word doesn't exist! I had to input the name into my spell check. Now, "thy kingdom come" implies that the kingdom is not the possession of man but the instrument of God. You must invite the kingdom rule of God into your life. You must input the rule of God to come into the computer of your heart. And until this is deliberately done you will never get over yourself.

"Thy will be done"

Again, there is the sense in which God is inviting you and me to call upon Him in order that His agenda is activated in any given situation. In Revelation 11:15, notice that the seventh trumpet has sounded, this is the last one to sound. Seven is symbolic of perfection, and here represents God's perfected will being manifested in the earth. Some translations say, "The kingdoms of this world are become" (KJV), or "has become" (NAS), "The kingdom of the world has become the kingdom of our Lord and of his Christ, and He will reign for ever and ever" (NIV). The form of the Greek is in the aroist tense, which conveys a sense of absolute certainty about the event yet to come. In other words, we don't see it as a present reality but it will occur! Now, what are the kingdoms of this world? Allow me to suggest just a few examples:

- Entertainment
- Sports
- Politics
- Economics
- Education

We must establish a Christian influence within the afore-mentioned kingdoms. I believe God's intent is for these king-doms to become the kingdom of Jesus Christ. Christ's influence must be felt beyond the four walls of the church. Thy will be done where? On earth as well as in heaven.

Now, my friend, something powerful happens when the seventh trumpet sounds. Paul said in 1 Corinthians 15:51–52, "Behold, I tell you a mystery: We shall not all sleep, but we shall all be changed—in a moment, in the twinkling of an eye, at the last trumpet. For the trumpet will sound, and the dead will be raised incorruptible, and we shall be changed." Paul said in 1 Thessalonians 4:16, "For the Lord Himself will descend from heaven with a shout, with the voice of an archangel, and with the trumpet of God. And the dead in Christ will rise first." Please indulge the preacher in me for a moment...that's why I've got a feeling that everything is going to be all right! Because when I think of the goodness of Jesus and all He's done for me, my soul cries out *Hallelujah, thank God for saving me!* I can hear the seventh trumpet sounding, can you?

That's why Psalm 24:7–8 says, "Lift up your heads, O you gates! And be lifted up, you everlasting doors! And the King of glory shall come in. Who is this King of glory? The LORD strong and mighty." "Thy kingdom come, thy will be done" (Matt. 6:10, KJV). It reminds me of movie advertisers who will show highlights of upcoming movies; usually all the action, and romantic scenes to get you to buy a ticket to see the movie. What type of highlights are you showing to peo-ple around you?

The first petition of the model prayer is "thy kingdom come, thy will be done." Is this your first petition? The main point I am striving to convey is this: the secret to getting over yourself is to live under the kingdom rule of God. Recently a member of the church where I am the pastor gave this heart-warming story. Although the circumstances may have been altered through the retelling of this story over time, it still illustrates an important point.

As she stood in front of her 5th grade class on the very first day of school, she told the children an untruth. Like most teachers, she looked at her students and said that she loved them all the same. However, that was impossible, because there in the front row, slumped in his seat, was a little boy named Teddy Stoddard.

Mrs. Thompson had watched Teddy the year before and noticed that he did not play well with the other children, that his clothes were messy, and that he constantly needed a bath. In addition, Teddy could be unpleasant. It got to the point where Mrs. Thompson would actually take delight in marking his papers with a broad red pen, making bold X's and then putting a big "F" at the top of his papers.

At the school where Mrs. Thompson taught, she was required to review each child's past records and she put Teddy's off until last. However, when she reviewed his file, she was in for a surprise.

Teddy's first grade teacher wrote, "Teddy is a bright child with a ready laugh. He does his work neatly and has good manners... he is a joy to be around."

His second grade teacher wrote, "Teddy is an excellent student, well liked by his classmates, but he is troubled because his mother has a terminal illness and life at home must be a struggle."

His third grade teacher wrote, "His mother's death has been hard on him. He tries to do his best, but his father doesn't show much interest, and his home life will soon affect him if some steps aren't taken."

By now, Mrs. Thompson realized the problem and she was ashamed of herself. She felt even worse when her students brought her Christmas presents, wrapped in beautiful ribbons and bright paper, except for Teddy's. His present was clumsily wrapped in the heavy, brown paper that he got from a grocery bag. Mrs. Thompson took pains to open it in the middle of the other presents. Some of the children started to laugh when she found a rhinestone bracelet with some of the stones missing, and a bottle that was one-quarter full of perfume. But she stifled the children's laughter when she exclaimed how pretty the bracelet was, putting it on, and dabbing some of the perfume on her wrist. Teddy Stoddard stayed after school that day just long enough to say, "Mrs. Thompson, today you smelled just like my Mom used to."

A year later, she found a note under her door, from Teddy, telling her that she was the best teacher he ever had in his whole life.

Six years went by before she got another note from Teddy. He then wrote that he had finished high school, third in his class, and she was still the best teacher he ever had in life.

Four years after that, she got another letter, saying that while things had been tough at times, he'd stayed in school, had stuck with it, and would soon graduate from college with the highest of honors. He assured Mrs. Thompson that she was still the best and favorite teacher he had ever had in his whole life.

Then four more years passed and yet another letter came. This time he explained that after he got his bachelor's degree, he decided to go a little further. The letter explained that she was still the best and favorite teacher he ever had. But now his name was a little longer... the letter was signed, Theodore F. Stoddard, MD.

The story does not end there. You see, there was yet another letter that spring. Teddy said he had met this girl and was going to be married. He explained that his father had died a coupled of years ago and he was wondering if Mrs. Thompson might agree to sit at the wedding in the place that was usually reserved for the mother of the groom. Of course, Mrs. Thompson did. And guess what? She wore that bracelet, the one with several rhinestones missing. Moreover, she made sure she was wearing the perfume that Teddy remembered his mother wearing on their last Christmas together.

They hugged each other, and Dr. Stoddard whispered in Mrs. Thompson's ear, "Thank you Mrs. Thompson for believing in me. Thank you so much for making me feel important and showing me that I could make a difference."

Mrs. Thompson, with tears in her eyes, whispered back. She said, "Teddy, you have it all wrong. You were the one who taught me that I could make a difference. I didn't know how to teach until I met you."

Thus, the obvious point of this illustration is that Mrs. Thompson got over herself and began to teach children. In so doing she made an impact upon the life of one child, Teddy.

Finally, Some Thoughts Why the Kingdom Doesn't Impact Believers As It Should

Why do your disciples transgress the tradition of the elders? For they do not wash their hands when they eat bread.... [then Jesus answered them] "Thus you have made the commandment of God of no effect by your tradition."

—MATTHEW 15:2, 6

The forces that hinder us from fully grasping the kingdom are our pride and man-made traditions and rituals. It is unfortunate that in some circles of the church, tradition is stronger than the authority of God's Word! The kingdom requires change:

Personal change

- Conduct

- Attitude
- Character

Church practices

- The way we do things
- Why we do what we do
- How we do what we do

The difference between tradition and traditionalism:

- Tradition is the dynamic practice of people attempting to live out their present history before God.

- Traditionalism is the dead practice of people attempting to live out their past history in the presence of men.

Traditionalism will always be the enemy of progress in the kingdom of God. One of my old homiletics' professors used to say, "We need to reach back only to grab the fire from the past and not the ashes." Along this line, I like what historian Jaroslav Pelican said, "Tradition is the living faith of the dead; traditionalism is the dead faith of the living."[5] Somehow, some way, get over yourself and learn what it means to live with purpose in the kingdom of God. Once again, the secret to getting over yourself is to live under the kingdom rule of God, and this will take true humility.

NOTES

⟫━◆━⟪

Introduction

1. George E. Ladd, *A Theology of The New Testament* (Grand Rapids, MI: Eerdmans, 1974) 105–119.

Chapter 1
God Has a Kingdom

1. Robert Bretall, editor, *A Kierkegaard Anthology* (New York: Random House, 1946), 293.

2. *The American Heritage Dictionary* (Boston: Houghton Mifflin Company, 1976).

3. *Scofield Reference Bible* (New York: Oxford University Press, Inc., 1909).

4. *Scofield Reference Bible* (New York: Oxford University Press, Inc., 1967) 1002.

Chapter 2
Employee's Handbook of the Kingdom

1. Alan E. Nelson, *Embracing Brokenness* (Colorado Springs, CO: NavPress, 2002), 59.

2. John MacArthur, Jr., *The MacArthur New Testament Commentary*, Matthew 1–7 (Chicago, IL: Moody Press, 1985), 131.

3. Poem available on the Internet at http://www.worldofquotes .com/author/Robert-Browning-Hamilton/1/index.html (accessed May 26, 2006).

4. William J. Henry, "The Highway of the King," 1911, public domain.

5. Patsy Clairmont, *Sportin' A Tude* (Colorado Springs, CO: Focus on the Family, 1996).

Chapter 3
Love One Another

1. C.S. Lewis, *Mere Christianity* (San Francisco: HarperSanFrancisco, 2001).

2. D.B. Towner and John Henry Sammis, "Trust and Obey," 1887, public domain.

3. Charles Wesley, "Jesus, Lord, We Look to Thee," 1749, public domain.

4. Orla C. Shup Albion, "How Do You Play That?" *Today's Christian Woman* (July–August 1994): 338.

Chapter 4
Get Over Yourself

1. Dietrich Bonhoeffer, *The Cost of Discipleship* (New York: Simon & Schuster, 1995).

2. Larry Crabb, *Connecting* (Nashville, TN: Word, 1997), xi.

3. Kevin Leman, *Winning the Rat Race Without Becoming a Rat* (Nashville, TN: Thomas Nelson, Pub. 1996), 222.

Chapter 5
I Love You and There's Nothing
You Can Do About It

1. Alan E. Nelson, *Embracing Brokenness* (Colorado Springs, CO: NavPress, 2002).

2. *Sermons Illustrated*, vol. 11, no. 6.90.

3. Philip P. Bliss, "Jesus Loves Even Me," public domain.

4. Howard E. Smith and James Rowe, "Love Lifted Me," public domain.

5. Statement by Mother Theresa, *Peace Making Day by Day*, Pax Christi, USA.

Chapter 6
No Time for Faultfinding

1. Quote available on the Internet at http://www.brainyquote .com/quotes/quotes/a/aeschylus148591.html.

2. John MacArthur, Jr., *The MacArthur New Testament Commentary*, Matthew 1–7 (Chicago, IL, Moody Press, 1985).

3. Eugene Peterson, *The Message* (Colorado Springs, CO: Nav-Press, 2002).

4. Coretta Scott King, editor, *The Words of Martin Luther King, Jr.* (New York: New Market Press, 1987), 17.

Chapter 7
You Must Be Born "Over Again"

1. Alan E. Nelson, *Embracing Brokenness*.

2. John Wesley, *The New Birth* (New York: Harper and Row Pub.), 6–7.

3. "Unconscious America," *Washington Times*.

4. Wesley, *The New Birth*, 11.

5. Elvina M. Hall, "Jesus Paid It All," 1865, public domain.

Chapter 8
The Kingdom Comes in a Seed

1. Alan E. Nelson, *Embracing Brokenness*.

2. John Cawood, "Almighty God, Thy Word Is Cast," 1819, public domain.

Chapter 9
Tribulation: Doorway to the Kingdom

1. Coretta Scott King, editor, *The Words of Martin Luther King, Jr.* (New York: Newmarket Press, 1987).

2. T.S. Eliot, *Christianity and Culture* (New York: Harcourt, 1976).

3. "Just Another Day That the Lord Has Kept Me," composer unknown, public domain.

4. "I Won't Complain," composer unknown, public domain.

5. *Sermons Illustrated*, Sept/Oct 1996, vol. 11.

Chapter 10
The Kingdom Is in the Holy Spirit

1. Quote available on the Internet at http://www.unca.edu/leadership/knowQuotations.html (accessed 5/29/06).

2. Myles Monroe, *Rediscovering the Kingdom* (Shippensburg, PA: Destiny, 2004) 32.

3. See *Fire on the Earth*, edited by Dr. Eddie Hyatt (Lake Mary, FL: Creation House, 2006).

4. *Aesop's Fables* (New York: Nelson Doubleday, 1968).

5. Frances R. Havergal, "Live Out Thy Life Within Me," 1864, public domain.

Chapter 11
Seek First the Kingdom

1. Fyodor Dostoyevsky, *The Brothers Karamazov* (New York: Bantam Books, 1970), 95.

2. Quote available on the Internet at http://www.quoteworld.org/quotes/8804 (accessed 5/29/06).

Chapter 12
What Do You Do When You Get Angry?

1. William H. Grier and Price M. Cobbs, *Black Rage* (New York: Bantan Books, 1968).

2. *Merriam-Webster's New Collegiate Dictionary* (6th Edition).

3. Gary Chapman, *The Other Side of Love: Handling Anger in a Godly Way* (Chicago, IL: Moody Press, 1999), 25.

4. "Dear Abby," *St. Paul Pioneer Press Dispatch*, June 5, 1990.

Chapter 13
Forgiving: It's in Your Best Interest

1. Quote available on the Internet at http://en.thinkexist .com/quotation/coming_together_is_a_beginning-keeping _together/146314.html (accessed 5/29/06).

2. Jerry Cook, *Love, Acceptance, and Forgiveness* (Ventura, CA: Regal Books, 1919), 11.

3. Lewis B. Smedes, *Forgive and Forget* (New York: Harper and Row Pub., 1984), 2.

4. George Nelson Allen and Thomas Shepherd, "Must Jesus Bear the Cross Alone?" public domain.

Epilogue: Nine Practical Principles on How to "Get Over Yourself"

1. Ted W. Engstrom, *The Making of a Christian Leader* (Grand Rapids, MI: Zondervan, 1976), 112.

2. Watchman Nee, *Spiritual Authority* (New York: Christian Fellowship Pub., INC., 1972), 115.

3. Howard A. Snyder, *A Kingdom Manifesto* (Downers Grove, IL: Inter Varsity Press, 1985), 57–58.

Final Words

1. Quote available on the Internet at http://www.teachnet .com/speakout/inspiration/index.html (accessed 5/29/06).

2. Jaroslav Pelikan, *Jesus Through the Centuries* (New York: Harper and Row, 1985), 73.